Spanish Memory Book

Spanish Memory Book

A New Approach to Vocabulary Building

by William F. Harrison
and Dorothy Winters Welker

University of Texas Press, Austin

First Edition, 1990

Requests for permission to reproduce material from this
work should be sent to Permissions, University of Texas
Press, Box 7819, Austin, Texas 78713-7819.

∞ The paper used in this publication meets the mini-
mum requirements of American National Standard for In-
formation Sciences—Permanence of Paper for Printed
Library Materials, ANSI Z39.48-1984.

Library of Congress Cataloging-in-Publication Data

Harrison, William F., 1934–
  Spanish memory book : a new approach to vocabulary
building / by William F. Harrison and Dorothy Winters
Welker. — 1st ed.
     p.   cm.
  ISBN 0-292-77640-3 (alk. paper). —
  ISBN 0-292-77641-1 (pbk. : alk. paper)
  1. Spanish language—Vocabulary. I. Welker, Dorothy
Winters, 1905– . II. Title.
PC4445.H37   1990
468.1—dc20   90-34146
                                                  CIP

Contents

To the Reader

IN LEARNING A new language, one of your first goals is to acquire a large stock of useful words in that language. The *Spanish Memory Book* is designed to help you learn Spanish words easily and fast and to recall them at will. It will enable you to recognize Spanish words when you see or hear them (passive vocabulary) and to recall these words when you speak or write Spanish (active vocabulary).

The *Spanish Memory Book* accomplishes this by means of mnemonic devices (memory helps). Mnemonic devices are not new, of course. They have been used for centuries. We still call upon them every day to remember names, numbers, and many other things. The mnemonic device sets up an association between a new word and old words that enables us to recall the new word. The mnemonic devices used in the *Spanish Memory Book* are rhymes that help you to remember both the pronunciation of the Spanish words and their English meanings. They fairly jingle the new words into your memory.

Research has shown, surprisingly enough, that the more far-fetched, even absurd, a mnemonic device is, the better it helps you remember. You will probably agree that many of the jingles in the *Spanish Memory Book* qualify for high marks in absurdity. You will have a good time learning and applying them.

The *Spanish Memory Book* contains about 700 words that were selected (with half a dozen exceptions) from the 2,000 most useful words in Spanish. (These words are listed in order of usefulness in the *Graded Spanish Wordbook*, compiled by Milton A. Buchanan, 3d ed. [Toronto: University of Toronto Press, 1941]).

How to Use the
Spanish Memory Book

READ THE SPANISH entry and the corresponding jingle, thus:

bailar   *to dance*   **Buy lar**ger shoes ┃ *to dance* ┃ in.
                                      Buy smaller pants to prance in.

The word to be learned is *bailar*, English "to dance." Incorporated in the jingle are English sounds that resemble the sounds of Spanish *bailar*. These sounds are *buy lar* and are printed in boldface type. Pronounce the boldfaced syllables carefully, making sure you pronounce them exactly as you pronounce them in English. Then note the corresponding English words ("to dance"), which are also incorporated in the jingle and are enclosed in a box.

    Now look away from the book and ask yourself, What is the English word for *bailar*? Chances are you will come up at once with "to dance." If not, just read the jingle once more.

    Shall we do another word?

frío   *cold*   **Free o**ld Tom from this ┃ *cold* ┃ world.
                                        His day is done, his flag is furled.

Here English *free o* gives the sound of Spanish *frío*. The English equivalent is "cold."

    And here is one more. Do it on your own.

barato   *cheap, in-*   **Bar Otto** from this ┃ *cheap* ┃ canteen
          expensive   Where fewer drinks than drunks are seen.

Conventions Used in This Book

1. As far as possible, the jingles reproduce the exact sounds of the Spanish words. When exactitude is not possible, the Spanish syllables are approximated. For the fine points of pronunciation, turn to a Spanish textbook or to your Spanish teacher. A table of pronunciations is provided in this book as a convenient reference.

2. The English equivalent of the Spanish word may appear in a jingle in any convenient form. For example, a verb may be in any tense. A noun may be either singular or plural. The main Spanish entry (alphabetical) always gives the infinitive of verbs and the singular of nouns.

3. The gender of nouns is given except for nouns ending in *o*, which are usually masculine, or in *a*, usually feminine. Endings are given for adjectives that indicate gender by *o* and *a*.

4. To make possible the inclusion of many Spanish words containing the sound *a* (English h*o*t, f*a*ther), the *Memory Book* occasionally replaces this sound by one of two similar sounds: ə (English *a*bout) or ɔ (English c*au*ght). This liberty has been taken only in unstressed syllables.

5. In the jingles, a long dash indicates a change of speaker.

Note: The *Memory Book* is aimed primarily at helping you learn vocabulary. It cannot give conjugations of verbs or rules of sentence structure. To do so would reduce the number of words that could be included and would encroach on the territory of language teachers and grammar textbooks.

Pronunciation

THIS SECTION IS included to serve as a reference in case you wish to refresh your memory of the basic rules of Spanish pronunciation.

Vowels* and Diphthongs

Spanish	English Approximation
a	*a* in f*a*ther
ai/ay	*aye*
au	t*ow*n
e	t*a*ke
ei/ey	w*eigh*; similar to Spanish *e*, but longer
i	mach*i*ne
io/yo	*yo*ke
o	n*o*
oi/oy	b*oy*
u	S*u*san; silent between *g* and *i*, between *g* and *e*, and after *q*
uo	*wo*e
ua	*wa*ter
ue	*wa*y

*Spanish single vowel sounds are always short and tense.

Consonants

b/v	*b*anana at the beginning of a sentence or of a word-group within a sentence and after *m* or *n*; elsewhere the lips barely meet
c	*c*at before *a*, *o*, *u*, or a consonant *s*at before *i* or *e*
ch	*ch*art
d	*d*og at the beginning of a sentence or of a word-group within the sentence and following *n* or *l*; elsewhere *d* approximates the *th* in *th*ey
f	*f*in
g	*g*o before *a*, *o*, *u* strongly aspirated *h* before *i* and *e*
h	always silent
j	strongly aspirated *h*
l	*l*ittle
ll	*y*es; *all* is pronounced *aye*
m	*m*other
n	like English *n* except preceding *m*, *b*, and *v*, when it is pronounced *m*
ñ	ca*ny*on
p	s*p*y
q	*q* is always followed by silent *u*; the combination is pronounced like *k* in *k*ite
r	after *n* and *l* and at the beginning of a word *r* is trilled, resulting in a sound something like the one children produce in imitating a motor; elsewhere *r* approximates the *dd* in la*dd*er
rr	always trilled
s	*s*o
t	*t*ask
v	see b/v above
x	so*ck*s; in a few Indian words such as México and Oaxaca *x* is pronounced like a strongly aspirated *h*
y	*y* in *y*es; when *y* stands alone it approximates the *e* in *e*qual
z	*s*o

Spanish Memory Book

Vocabulary

Spanish	*English*	
abajo	*below,*	**Ah, bah! Jo**sé, don't look ⌐ *below* ⌐.
	down	Ignore the fear all climbers know.
abrazo	*hug,*	**A bra so** snug
	embrace	Invites a ⌐ *hug* ⌐.
abrir	*to open*	⌐ *To open* ⌐ the debating season
		B**ob rear**ed a monument to reason.
abuelo	*grandpa,*	**Bob, wail o**bediently at ⌐ *Grandpa* ⌐'s grave.
	grandfather	Never admit you knew him to be a knave.
acabar de	*to have*	Kn**ock a bar they** won't let ladies drink in.
	just	—That's the very thing I ⌐ *'ve just* ⌐ been thinkin'.
acaso	*perhaps*	Pea**cock, ah! So** gorgeous is your train
		⌐ *Perhaps* ⌐ we can forget your tiny brain.
		(But why do peacocks make me think of Jane?)
aceite (m.)	*oil*	**Pa, say te**quila made that ugly spot.
		Some olive ⌐ *oil* ⌐ will cure it, like as not.

acera	*sidewalk*	**Ah, Sarah**, keep the ⌈ *sidewalk* ⌉ neat. Walk your dog along the street.
acertar	*to hit upon*	**R**oss, **air Tar**zan's dark and shameful deed, Then ⌈ *hit upon* ⌉ a way to make him bleed.
acoger	*to harbor, greet, receive, shelter*	**Pa, coher**ence is a virtue. ⌈ *Harbor* ⌉ it; it will not hurt you.
acostarse	*to go to bed*	**Ah, co-star, say** now goodnight. Let's ⌈ *go to bed* ⌉ —we're all so tight.
actual- mente	*nowadays, at present*	⌈ *Nowadays* ⌉ (not out of goodness of heart) The boss gives a cl**ock to all men ta**king part.
acuerdo	*agreement, resolution*	We must, J**ock, wear tho**se muddy army boots. It's our ⌈ *agreement* ⌉ with the raw recruits.
¡adelante!	*go ahead! forward!*	**Pa, they'll on te**quila sup, So ⌈ *go ahead* ⌉ and fill your cup.
ademán (m.)	*gesture, attitude*	My pa and m**a, they mon**itor with care My speech, my ⌈ *gestures* ⌉, and my underwear.
adentro	*inside*	**A then Tro**jan warrior was eyeing the horse. ⌈ *Inside* ⌉ were some Greeks, who were hiding, of course.
adiós	*good-bye*	**Ah! the oh s**o lovely child! She said ⌈ *good-bye* ⌉ and sweetly smiled.
afán (m.)	*zeal*	Laur**a, fon**d of roasted eel, Prepared it with her wonted ⌈ *zeal* ⌉.
agente (m.)	*agent*	Will **a hen ta**ke her ⌈ *agent* ⌉ to court For cutting her tail feathers short?

agotar	*to drain, exhaust*	**Ah, go tar** and feather reckless rabble Who ⟨ *drain* ⟩ our patience with their endless babble.
agregar	*to add*	**Pa, gray guar**d of all my drinking, Can you ⟨ *add* ⟩ sense to what I'm thinking?
agua	*water*	Man**agua** ⟨ *water* ⟩ tastes like death. That's why there's whiskey on my breath.
ahí	*there*	**Ah! Ea**st is ⟨ *there* ⟩ and West is here, And each of us finds the other queer.
ahogar	*to drown*	**Pa, oh guar**d the old mill pool. A child ⟨ *was drowned* ⟩ there after school.
ahora	*now*	**Ah! Ora** will be more than happy ⟨ *now* ⟩; For Christmas she received a lovely sow.
aire (m.)	*air*	An **ira**te pilot high in ⟨ *air* ⟩ Lost his temper and bombed the fair.
ajeno, -a	*foreign, alien*	**Ah, hay no** way is ⟨ *foreign* ⟩ to a horse, But Mama served it for our second course!
ala	*wing*	**D**oll**a**rs are the magic ⟨ *wings* ⟩ That turn our *wishes* into *things.*
alabar	*to praise*	**Allah bar**s his followers from liquor, And yet the vintners ⟨ *praise* ⟩ him while they dicker.
alcanzar	*to reach (a place)*	At last the **B**al**kan ser**geant ⟨ *reached* ⟩ his goal, But never could pronounce Sebastopol.
alegre	*happy, merry*	**A leg Ray** is ⟨ *happy* ⟩ to bare Is tattooed with the head of his mare.

alemán (m.)	*German*	**All a mon**ocled $\boxed{\textit{German}}$ can think of to do Is to stare out of one eye and not out of two.
algo	*some-thing*	**Moll go**es crazy when she thinks Tom put $\boxed{\textit{something}}$ in her drinks.
alguno, -a	*some*	**All goon? No** way. $\boxed{\textit{Some}}$ say it's so, But Herman's only dull and slow.
aliento	*courage, breath*	Trust me, **Ollie, ento**mology Needs more $\boxed{\textit{courage}}$ than apology.
alimentar	*to feed*	**Ollie meant Ar**thur $\boxed{\textit{to feed}}$ her pet cat, But Arthur likes cat food, the treacherous brat.
alimento	*food*	**Ollie meant—oh,** foolish attitude! She much prefers desserts to solid $\boxed{\textit{food}}$.
alma	*soul*	**C**alm **a** $\boxed{\textit{soul}}$ by talk of Paradise, And say you find your heaven in her eyes.
alzar	*to raise, elevate*	Op**al, sor**ry for her escapades, When dressing $\boxed{\textit{will}}$ no longer $\boxed{\textit{raise}}$ the shades.
allí	*there*	**Aye, ye** are sinners kneeling $\boxed{\textit{there}}$, But why not put on underwear?
amar	*to love*	Who $\boxed{\textit{loves}}$ a **mar**tyr loves a fool, So calm your ardor, keep your cool.
ambos, -as	*both*	**Tom boas**ts happily that he's a twin. They $\boxed{\textit{both}}$ were born to fight, and one to win.
amenazar	*to threaten*	**Ah, men, a sor**ry lot you seem to be. When danger $\boxed{\textit{threatens}}$, you just climb a tree.
amigo	*friend*	**Ah me, go** home at last, my $\boxed{\textit{friend}}$. I see you've no more cash to spend.

amo	landlord, master, owner	On Christmas Day we'll b**omb o**ld Scrooge's place. As ⟦ *landlord* ⟧ he has proved a sheer disgrace.
amor (m.)	love	**A mor**tal wholly lacking ⟦ *love* ⟧ Is like a hand without a glove.
ancho, -a	wide	The swamp that **Pancho** tried to pass Is ⟦ *wide* ⟧ and full of deadly gas.
andar	to walk	**On Dar**tmouth campus once I ⟦ *walked* ⟧. I liked the way the students talked.
ansia	anxiety	Did **Don see a** ghost, in a fit of ⟦ *anxiety* ⟧? Or was it a vision, reward of true piety?
año	year	Press **on, Yo**landa. Just a few more sprints And you'll be seen in this ⟦ *year* ⟧'s racing prints.
apagar	to turn off	Our p**apa guar**ds his children's health And ⟦ *turns off* ⟧ lights to save their wealth.
apartar	to separate	**Ah, part Ar**thur from his stormy mate. ⟦ *Separate* ⟧ them ere it is too late.
apenas	hardly, scarcely	**A pain as**sures me I am still alive But that I'm ⟦ *hardly* ⟧ eager to survive.
apoyar	to support	Gest**apo yar**ns ⟦ *support* ⟧ the monstrous claim That Nazis never did those deeds of shame.
aprender	to learn	A t**op wren dare**s, no doubt, ⟦ *to learn* ⟧ To fly to France when it comes her turn.
apretar	to squeeze	Pa**, pray tar** and feather those Who ⟦ *squeeze* ⟧ us into small-size clothes.
apro-vechar	to take advantage of	**Ah, probe a char**t and find a treasure hid. Then ⟦ *take advantage of* ⟧ the highest bid.

apurar	*to speed up, hurry, press*	**Ah, poor Ar**thur! ⬚ Speed ⬚ him ⬚ up ⬚. He stops to pet each mongrel pup.
aquel	*that (over yonder)*	⬚ That ⬚ book over yonder belongs to R**aquel**. If you have torn it you'd better not tell.
aquí	*here*	**Ah, key** your spending to your wages, And you will flourish ⬚ here ⬚ for ages.
árbol (m.)	*tree*	Greta G**arbo l**ies beneath this ⬚ tree ⬚. I wish I thought her dreams were all of me.
arder	*to burn*	I know you ⬚ burn ⬚ to, but you simply can't B**ar their** gross presence from my maiden aunt.
arma	*gun, arm, weapon*	We'll **arm a** nation with tanks and ships And pile up ⬚ guns ⬚ till the enemy flips.
arre-pentirse	*to repent*	**Ah, Ray, pen**t tear**s say** you at last ⬚ repent ⬚, Recalling things you said but never meant.
arriba	*upstairs, up*	**Ah, Reba**, Reba, where on earth is Reba? —She's gone ⬚ upstairs ⬚ to spank our little Sheba.
arrojar	*to throw*	P**a, row har**d to port. I ⬚ 'll throw ⬚ a line To that poor fellow struggling in the brine.
así	*thus, so*	M**a, see** the rapidly approaching bus. It may not stop if you keep screaming ⬚ thus ⬚.
asiento	*seat*	**Ah, see ento**mologists explore The cracks in every crumbling ⬚ seat ⬚ and floor.
asistir	*to attend, be present*	Hur**rah! See steer**s ⬚ attend ⬚ the meeting. Hear the cows all low their greeting.
asomar	*to come into view, begin to appear*	**Ah, so mar**velous it was—on cue The Stars and Stripes ⬚ came ⬚ floating ⬚ into view. ⬚

aspecto	*appear-ance*	**A speck to**ld the doctor I'd injured my eye. Its appearance improved when he doused it with rye.
aspirar	*to inhale*	**Ah, spear Ar**thur. Better yet, Make him inhale a cigarette.
asunto	*affair, business*	**Ah, soon To**más will wind up his affairs. No one will wonder why, for no one cares.
asustar	*to frighten*	**Pa, Sue star**s in many a gangster movie. It frightens me, but she declares it's groovy.
atar	*to tie up, tie*	The cops g**ot Tar**zan. First they tied him up, But later found him harmless as a pup.
atrás	*behind, back*	The cop g**ot Ros**coe by his long black braid. I slipped behind and socked him with a spade.
atravesar	*to cross*	**Dot, rob a ser**geant or outwit a colonel, And cross for once that status-gap eternal.
atreverse	*to dare*	**Ah, Tray, bear Se**lina's constant teasing. Ere long I dare to think you'll find it pleasing.
aumento	*increase*	A sudden increase in the population **N**ow **meant (oh**, dreadful thought!) increased taxation.
aunque	*though, although*	Though loved by all the **town, Kay** has a quirk: She tends to go to sleep while others work.
aurora	*dawn*	**N**ow **roar a**while, and get it off your chest. When comes the dawn, you'll find your ma knows best.
ave (f.)	*bird*	Rely on my word: B**ob a**te our bird. You say he's a bird lover? Simply absurd!

averiguar	*to find out, ascertain*	**A berry goo Ar**thur had spilled on his pants, As he quickly ⌐*found out*⌐, had attracted some ants.
ayer	*yesterday*	**"Aye, air** on earth," the scientist affirms, "Just ⌐*yesterday*⌐ was free of germs."
azúcar (m.)	*sugar*	**A Sioux car**eened into yonder shelf, Opened the ⌐*sugar*⌐ , and helped himself.
azul	*blue*	**A Sioux'll** be there when the fun begins, Wearing his ⌐*blue*⌐ fur moccasins.

B

Spanish	*English*	
bailar	*to dance*	**Buy lar**ger shoes ⌐*to dance*⌐ in; Buy smaller pants to prance in.
bajar	*to get off, descend*	Dear old Ab**ba har**dly made a sound When, tottering, he ⌐*got off*⌐ the merry-go-round.
bajo, -a	*low, short*	My score was ⌐*low*⌐ on the medical test. —**Bah! Ho**me remedies work out best.
bañar	*to bathe*	Dau**b on yar**ds of finest silk Shapes of goblins and their ilk. Then ⌐*bathe*⌐ in spice the local queen And wrap her up for Halloween.

barba	*beard*	A **barba**rous practice, greatly feared, Is shaving off a convict's ⟨ *beard* ⟩ .
barco	*ship, boat*	**Bar co**caine from every ⟨ *ship* ⟩ And stash a gun on every hip.
bastar	*to be enough*	Ab**ba star**red—and flopped—in his own show. That ⟨ *was enough* ⟩ to use up all his dough.
batir	*to beat*	**Bah! Tear**s will never help your case. Just ⟨ *beat* ⟩ your drum in the boss's face.
beber	*to drink*	Give the **babe air**, make her ⟨ *drink* ⟩ water. After all, boys, she's somebody's daughter.
bendecir	*to bless*	**Ben, day ser**ials we have ⟨ *to bless* ⟩ : A "soap" can save a soul from loneliness.
besar	*to kiss*	**Base ar**guments are sure to well From lips that mean ⟨ *to kiss* ⟩ and tell.
beso	*kiss*	Smart little maidens should always o**bey. So** Give me a ⟨ *kiss* ⟩ and I'll give you a peso.
bien	*fine, well*	The season would **be en**ding ⟨ *fine* ⟩ If you would be my valentine.
blanco, -a	*white*	Cale**b, Lon co**-chaired the ⟨ *White* ⟩ House group. The chief of staff got soused, and flew the coop.
boca	*mouth*	A **beau co**llapsed somewhere down south: His girlfriend slapped him in the ⟨ *mouth* ⟩ .
boda	*wedding*	**Bo, the** ⟨ *wedding* ⟩ plans are set. See my shotgun? Pay your debt!
bondad	*kindness, goodness*	With large-boned girls their ⟨ *kindness* ⟩ coos and coddles. The small-**boned—ah! th**ey serve as artist's models.

bonito, -a   *pretty*   Is Ram**bo neat or** slightly nutty?
—He's just a ⬚ *pretty* ⬚ piece of putty.

borde (m.)   *verge, edge,*   That **bore, they** say, has proved of no utility.
          border   His speech was on the ⬚ *verge* ⬚ of sheer futility.

borrar   *to erase*   Our men **bore ar**tifacts. We scanned in haste
The glyphs that carried symbols half ⬚ *erased* ⬚ .

bosque   *woods,*   Don't be ver**bose, Kay**. But you must explain
(m.)   *forest*   How in the ⬚ *woods* ⬚ you lost your hydroplane.

brazo   *arm*   A **bra so** tight it might do harm
Had best be worn about the ⬚ *arm* ⬚ .

broma   *joke*   Je**b, Roma** played a ⬚ *joke* ⬚ on local Arabs:
She somehow sold them all synthetic scarabs.

brotar   *to bud*   Bo**b wrote Tar**zan in his own red blood:
"The seeds of vengeance ever swell and ⬚ *bud* ⬚ ."

burla   *joke, trick*   He's a **boor. Lo**p off his ugly nose.
(It's just a ⬚ *joke* ⬚ : We'll only take his toes.)

burlar   *to scoff,*   Well, **boor, lar**ks like yours are getting pretty stale.
       mock   They start by ⬚ *scoffing* ⬚ , but they end in jail.

busca   *search*   Let's end the futile ⬚ *search* ⬚ for "maybes" and
"perhapses"
And plan what we can do when this ca**boose
co**llapses.

buscar   *to seek,*   Bam**boo scar**s are mostly not too serious.
       look for   But ⬚ *seek* ⬚ a doctor lest you get delirious.

C-CH

Spanish	English	
caber	*to fit into, be contained, fit*	The In**ca bur**ied his arrow and bow [**To fit into**] the world that white men know.
cabeza	*head*	Don't let the In**ca base a** camp Here where the ground is cold and damp. His [**head**] will ache, his legs will cramp.
caer	*to fall*	The In**ca er**ror was, they stopped to yell When Rabbit-in-the-Moon, their leader, [**fell**].
caja	*box*	Loo**k! ah, ho**t coffee! And a [**box**] Of the very best quality kosher lox!
calor (m.)	*heat, warmth*	The [**heat**]'s on. Fis**cal or**der is a must. So bring your files. But first, wipe off the dust.
cama	*bed*	A **comma** helps us get our sentence said. A period lets us spend our time in [**bed**].
cámara	*chamber, hall, parlor*	**Calm a ra**bbinical student who thinks The [**chamber**] he rented decidedly stinks.
cambiar	*to change*	Let **calm be Ar**thur's goal in life. He cannot [**change**] the world by strife.
camino	*road*	Your grave, **calm mien, O** creature born to beauty, Lights up the dismal [**road**] that leads to duty.

campo	*field,*	The **compo**st heap you put in yonder $\boxed{\textit{field}}$
	campus,	Offends the nose, but will increase our yield.
	country	

| cansar | *to tire* | It $\boxed{\text{tires}}$ me out to see the congregation |
| | | Applaud the i**con, Ser**geant Carr's creation. |

| cantar | *to sing* | Her smiles **con Tar**zan into $\boxed{\textit{singing}}$ |
| | | And start his great gorillas swinging. |

| canto | *song* | When **Kahn to**bogganed down that hill, |
| | | His tuneless $\boxed{\textit{song}}$ was sounding still. |

| capaz | *capable* | Foolish Dor**ca, pos**turing and prancing, |
| | | Believes she's $\boxed{\textit{capable}}$ of modern dancing. |

| cara | *face* | My **car a**gain has lost a race. |
| | | It just exploded in my $\boxed{\textit{face}}$. |

| cárcel (f.) | *jail* | Those who from a **car sell** drugs |
| | | Must go to $\boxed{\textit{jail}}$ like other thugs. |

| cargo | *load,* | I watched our **car go** limping with its $\boxed{\textit{load}}$. |
| | *burden* | It almost capsized when it hit a toad. |

| caricia | *petting,* | Why does **Carisse see a** possible ban on $\boxed{\textit{petting}}$? |
| | *tenderness* | —Because our town has such a romantic setting. |

cariño	*love,*	To show your $\boxed{\textit{love}}$, **careen Yo**landa's boat
	affection	and paint the hull.
		But guard it from the calling cards of every
		passing gull.

| carne (f.) | *meat* | The **car Na**te sold me smells of rancid $\boxed{\textit{meat}}$. |
| | | —He once sold hot dogs daily on the street. |

| carrera | *race* | Di**ck, a rare a**ttempt has just been made |
| | | To stage a rat $\boxed{\textit{race}}$ in the second grade. |

carro	*car, coach*	His **car** ro**lled over in the race. He was not hurt, but did lose face.
carta	*letter*	The mailman has to **cart a** lot of **letters** From creditors to unrepentant debtors.
casa	*house*	In my **house**, **Casa**blanca has become a daily thriller. The only thing the movie lacks is good old Phyllis Diller.
casi	*almost*	Dic**k, ah! see**s only the good that lies in man, So **almost** all of us cheat him whenever we can.
caso	*in case,* *case*	Dere**k, ah! so**le guardian of my heart, Tell me what to do **in case** we part.
ceder	*to yield,* *cede*	My friends **say they're** not sure there is a heaven, But I won't **yield** : I claim that there are seven.
celos (pl.)	*jealousy*	Reporters **say low-s**alaried bureaucrats Show **jealousy** of those who wear top hats.
cena	*supper*	**Say, Na**nette, before we go to **supper** Couldn't you mix us each a picker-upper?
ceniza	*ashes, ash*	**Say! Niece A**licia burned her house to **ashes**. —So what? The dear girl so enjoys her bashes.
cerca	*near*	Thi**s air ca**resses like a loving hand. The ocean's **near**. This is a favored land.
cerrar	*to close,* *fasten,* *lock*	The cor**sair ar**gued hotly while he drank: "The subject **'s closed** ; you'll have to walk the plank."
ciego, -a	*blind*	**See A go** stumbling wildly after B. So **blind** they are, they'll crash into the C.

cielo	*heaven, sky*	It seems we won't **see ale o**r beer in $\boxed{\textit{heaven}}$, So let's start now by downing six or seven.
cierto, -a	*certain*	Dar**cy, air to**bacco if you must. I'm $\boxed{\textit{certain}}$ folks will greet you with disgust.
cita	*appoint- ment, date*	Do **see to**p officers for an $\boxed{\textit{appointment}}$ To talk about your new reducing ointment.
claro, -a	*clear, light- colored*	With great é**clat Ro**berta chaired the meeting. It's $\boxed{\textit{clear}}$ the opposition was but fleeting.
clase (f.)	*class*	The $\boxed{\textit{class}}$ performed with great é**clat, say** many. But if you question *me*, they haven't any.
cobrar	*to collect*	$\boxed{\textit{Collect}}$ a Sex**co bra r**eplete with images Of co-eds taking part in football scrimmages.
cocer	*to cook*	**Coe, Sar**ah simply cannot sew or $\boxed{\textit{cook}}$. Her talent lies in leafing through a book.
coche (m.)	*car, coach*	The **coach a** king once rode in across the cobblestones Is in a $\boxed{\textit{car}}$ museum that will send it out on loans.
cocina	*kitchen*	This town's roco**co scene a**ppeals to people Who shun the $\boxed{\textit{kitchen}}$ but admire the steeple.
cólera	*anger*	**Cole, ere A**dele explodes in $\boxed{\textit{anger}}$ Hustle her off to her friends in Bangor.
colgar	*to hang*	**Cole, gar**ters aren't enough $\boxed{\textit{to hang}}$ yourself. You'll have to use the gun on that high shelf.
colocar	*to set, place*	**Cole, oak ar**bors are in fashion. They're A peaceful place $\boxed{\textit{to set}}$ your rocking chair.
comer	*to eat*	Bas**com, heir** to Grandpa's wealth, $\boxed{\textit{Ate}}$ all day and wrecked his health.

cometer	*to commit*	**Comb a ter**rorist and find a sadist. Of all bad actions, he ⟦ *commits* ⟧ the baddest.
comida	*meal*	I'm no co-worker. I'm just **co-me**. The ⟦ *meals* ⟧ I like are the ones served free.
cómo	*how*	**Comb O**phelia's hair and wash her face. Then ask her ⟦ *how* ⟧ she met with this disgrace.
conducir	*to lead, conduct*	**Cohn, do sear** the cornfields you traverse, And ⟦ *lead* ⟧ your army with a heartfelt curse.
conmover	*to rouse*	**Coe, mow bur**ial grounds with care. It's easy ⟦ *To rouse* ⟧ the rattlesnakes and make them queasy.
cono-cimiento	*acquain-tance*	**Coe, no seamy ento**mologist May claim ⟦ *acquaintance* ⟧ with the girls I've kissed.
consejo	*advice, counsel*	**Cohn, say Jo**sé gives good ⟦ *advice* ⟧. He still can't rid your pad of lice.
consuelo	*conso-lation, comfort*	**Cohn, sway Lo**rette to join our church society. It offers ⟦ *consolation* ⟧, peace, and piety.
contar	*to count*	Does showman Jac**k own tar**tan ballet skirts? —He ⟦ *counts* ⟧ five hundred, so the press asserts.
contestar	*to answer, reply*	**Cohn, test Ar**thur's readiness ⟦ *to answer* ⟧. —I've done so, and he stammers what he can, sir.
contra	*against*	The ice-cream **cone tra**versed a ten-inch gap And crashed ⟦ *against* ⟧ the flight commander's cap.
convenir	*to agree*	Ma**comb, Ben ir**ritates both you and me: The only thing on which we two ⟦ *agree* ⟧.

corazón (m.)	*heart*	Little **Cora, so n**aive and simple, Cried her ⟨ *heart* ⟩ out when she found a pimple.
corona	*crown*	Help the Peace **Corps own a** civic ⟨ *crown* ⟩ . They are the finest citizens in town.
correr	*to run*	**Core rare** ripe apples for the table, But ⟨ *run* ⟩ with green ones to the stable.
corriente	*common, current, standard*	The strange, dar**k Orient, a** world away, Is winning in the ⟨ *common* ⟩ game we play.
cortar	*to cut*	No en**core Tar**zan got: He⟨ *'d cut* ⟩ A scene notorious for its smut.
corte (m.)	*court*	Es**cort a** damsel to the ⟨ *court* ⟩ To watch the doughty knights cavort.
cosa	*thing*	Jo**cose a**llusions to sacred ⟨ *things* ⟩ Prick my patience like insect stings.
costa	*coast, cost*	Jo**cose Ta**llulah used to boast That she could swim from ⟨ *coast* ⟩ to coast.
crecer	*to grow*	Let's have a tal**k race, Sar**ah: As we ⟨ *grow* ⟩ We'll tell each other everything we know.
creer	*to think, believe*	Crac**k Ray air**ily over the head. When he wakes up he'll ⟨ *think* ⟩ he's dead.
criado, -a	*servant*	The young **Cree, ah! though** fit and fervent, Is much too proud to be a ⟨ *servant* ⟩ .
cruz (f.)	*cross*	A mini-**crew s**ufficed to ferry us. We brought no props but a ⟨ *cross* ⟩ to bury us.
cruzar	*to cross*	The flight **crew Ser**geant Smith engaged ⟨ *Have crossed* ⟩ the bridge to middle age.

cuál	*which*	Jack, wallabies are strange Australian creatures. — Which is the one you say has Papa's features?
cubrir	*to cover*	Your last **coup (Brie r**eplete with sherry) Covered the earth with dysentery.
cuenta	*bill,* *account*	Jack went a-fishing in the ocean, Brought back a bill for suntan lotion.
cuerpo	*body*	A s**quare po**sition is the best To give your battered body rest.
cuidar	*to look* *after, take* *care of*	Pa, be**queath ar**mor and horse to your sons. They can look after them. I'll take your guns.
culpa	*guilt*	**Cool Pa**'s extravagant feeling of guilt. He did drive the blade in, but not to the hilt.
chocar	*to clash, be* *shocking,* *collide*	The gau**cho car**ted coal and also cash, But never let these occupations clash.

Spanish	*English*	
daño	*loss,* *damage*	**Don, Yo**landa took a heavy loss When IRS descended on her boss.
dar	*to give*	**Dar**la, give to Tom your best, And leave to others all the rest.

deber (m.)	*debt, duty*	Some **day, bur**y thoughts of these old ⟨ **debts** ⟩ And learn to live untrammelled by regrets.
decir	*to say, tell*	One **day sear**ing tongues ⟨ *will say* ⟩ He should have died in a different way.
dedo	*finger, toe*	O'**Day, though** plainly loath to linger, Accepted rum—but just a ⟨ *finger* ⟩.
dedo	*toe, finger*	Each **day, though** chased by hoards of mice, We search our grimy ⟨ **toes** ⟩ for lice.
dejar	*to leave (behind), allow*	Some **day har**m will come to those Who ⟨ *leave* ⟩ unwashed their underclothes.
del	*from the, of the*	**Dell** ⟨ *from the* ⟩ well let out a yell. The echo returned like a voice from hell.
delito	*crime*	One **day Lee to**ld all about his ⟨ *crime* ⟩. Now he must stand his trial and serve his time.
depender	*to depend*	O'**Day, penned air**less in a crowded cell, ⟨ **Depends** ⟩ on us to make the treaty jell.
descuido	*neglect, care-lessness*	**Desk, we—though** both of us show some ⟨ *neglect* ⟩ — Still make a rather scholarly effect.
desear	*to want, desire, wish*	The boys each **day say ar**dent prayers: They ⟨ *want* ⟩ to meet the girls upstairs.
deseo	*desire*	Some **day, say o**ld, mystical predictions, ⟨ **Desire** ⟩ will end, along with fights and frictions.
despertar	*to waken*	⟨ *Waken* ⟩ **Dess, pare tar**tar off her teeth, And show the costly dentures underneath.

desprecio	*disdain, contempt*	**Dess, pray see o**ver the hedge and down the lane A moose observing us all with high $\boxed{\textit{disdain}}$.
detener	*to arrest, detain, stop*	To**day ten er**rant boys I saw buy drugs. $\boxed{\textbf{Arrest}}$ them, else tomorrow they'll be thugs.
detrás de	*behind, in back of*	I will **date Ross. They**'d better not tell Mabel. I guess we'll have to meet $\boxed{\textit{behind}}$ the stable.
día (m.)	*day*	New i**dea**s hit me every $\boxed{\textit{day}}$. Sometimes I almost wish they'd go away.
dicha	*good fortune, joy*	Melo**dy cha**-chas with every suitor. Her great $\boxed{\textit{good fortune}}$ is, they're getting cuter.
dichoso, -a	*happy*	I've sprea**d each oh-so**-dainty cracker With guava jelly smooth as lacquer, And now you see a $\boxed{\textit{happy}}$ snacker.
dinero	*money*	**Dean, aero**nautics could be my salvation. But how get $\boxed{\textit{money}}$ when I'm on probation? I dare not rob a single subway station.
dios	*god*	**Dee, oh s**o tried and true you seem to be. But darling, please don't make a $\boxed{\textit{god}}$ of me.
dirigir	*to steer, direct*	**Deary, hear** me when I plead: $\boxed{\textbf{Steer}}$ the boat but watch your speed.
disculpar	*to excuse*	**Dee, school par**ties $\boxed{\textit{do}}$ n't $\boxed{\textbf{excuse}}$ Your cutting class to take a snooze.
dolor (m.)	*pain*	I found **Dolor**es right as rain, Though she'd been having stomach $\boxed{\textit{pain}}$.
doloroso, -a	*mournful, sad*	The **dole, or oh! so** $\boxed{\textit{mournful}}$ faces, Will always tell of tragic cases.

dónde	*where*	Where do you think a physicist should start?
		—Well, to begin with he should **own De**scartes.

dormir	*to sleep*	This **door mere**ly leads to the castle keep.
		Our ghost lives there to haunt you while you
		sleep .

duda	*doubt*	I have no doubt you truly want to please,
		But please don't **do the** tango on your knees.

durante	*during*	The debt **due Ron ta**kes all my ready cash.
		So during March I dare not plan a bash.

duro, -a	*tough,*	**Do row** hard; the going's tough .
	hard	Call me when you've had enough.

Spanish	*English*	

echar	*to throw,*	When you, R**ay, char**t a course across the
	pour	Indian Ocean
		We'll all throw in our lot with you in dumb
		devotion.

ejercer	*to perform,*	G**ray hair Sar**ah views with growing spite.
	exercise	She now performs each week a dyeing rite.

él	*he*	He 's much too **el**egant to swear.
		He says that oaths get in his hair.

elegir	*to choose,*	Thank you. I shall choose , I think,
	elect	Old English **ale, a her**o's drink.

empezar	*to start, begin*	Cl**em, pay Ser**geant Black ⟦ ***to start*** ⟧ a war. Just let him wonder what he's fighting for.
empleo	*job*	Make th**em play "O**ld Oaken Bucket." That's their ⟦ ***job*** ⟧ and they can't duck it.
empujar	*to push*	Cl**em, pooh Har**vard, cheer your hometown team. Your faith can ⟦ ***push*** ⟧ them farther than they dream.
en	*at, in, on*	B**en** ⟦ ***at*** ⟧ gambling is a shark, But how he wins I'm ⟦ ***in*** ⟧ the dark.
encanto	*enchant-ment*	Wh**en Kahn to**ld fairy stories on the air, ⟦ ***Enchantment*** ⟧ held each kiddie in his chair. (Adults, however, left the room to swear.)
encargo	*order, com-mission*	"Light**en cargo"** is the captain's ⟦ ***order*** ⟧. We'll have to sacrifice our new recorder.
encender	*to kindle, light*	B**en, send Er**rol to the streets ⟦ ***to kindle*** ⟧ The people's wrath against the royal swindle.
encima	*above*	⟦ ***Above*** ⟧ , the gunm**en see ma**lignant powers Gathering force to capture what is ours.
enfermo, -a	*sick, ill*	Wh**en fair Mo**desta's dog was ⟦ ***sick*** ⟧ He sought his mistress' hand to lick.
engañar	*to deceive, trick*	B**en gone? Yar**ds of silk, too, I believe. I fear the villain practiced ⟦ ***to deceive*** ⟧.
enojo	*trouble, bother*	Wom**en know ho**me brew is too much ⟦ ***trouble*** ⟧. You have to sit for hours and watch it bubble.
enorme	*huge, big, large*	**A norm a** broker learns to follow Is: Take ⟦ ***huge*** ⟧ losses at a swallow.

en seguida	*at once*	When m**en say "ghee," the** sheikhs **at once** will mutter, "We know the stuff they serve is only butter."
entender	*to under-stand*	Wh**en ten dare to understand** , Nine will fight and one command.
enterar	*to inform*	B**en, tear Ar**thur quivering limb from limb. But first, **inform** us why you're down on him.
entero, -a	*whole, entire*	I saw B**en tear o**ld holly wreaths to pieces And burn **whole** Christmas trees before his nieces.
entonces	*then*	M**entone Cec**ilia found among the prime resorts, First for making love, and **then** for other sports.
entre	*between, among*	The m**en trai**led grimly, two by two, **Between** our stalwart boys in blue.
enviar	*to send*	When no cash was left **to send** , B**emby ar**gued with his friend.
envidiar	*to envy*	Clem, **be the Ar**gonaut you used to dream of. **Envy** no more that crowd you are the cream of.
época	*time, epoch*	Did R**ay poke a** thumb in your innocent face? It's a sign of the **time** and the man and the place.
equivocar	*to mistake, make a mistake*	**A key Bo car**ped about last night he merely **Mistook** for one he once had treasured dearly.
escalar	*to scale, climb surreptitiously*	B**ess, call Ar**t **to scale** the wall. We'll get out now or not at all.
escoger	*to choose*	Y**es, coher**ence is a virtue. If you **choose** it, it won't hurt you.

escribir	*to write*	Yes, **Cree beer** is always smooth and light. A pint or two will give me strength 〔**to write**〕.
escuchar	*to listen, listen to*	**Bess, coo char**ming songs into my ear And let me 〔**listen**〕 while I guzzle beer.
escuela	*school*	**Les, quail a** bully, flout a fool. They only need to go to 〔**school**〕.
esfera	*sphere*	**Less fair a** girl at once appeared to be When she declared her 〔**sphere**〕 included me.
espalda	*back*	Yes, **Paul, Da**kotas are at your 〔**back**〕. Hide in a wigwam before you crack.
espejo	*mirror*	**Less pay ho**lds out to us a dismal view, 〔**Mirror**〕 of misery for me and you.
esperanza	*hope*	End the str**ess. Pay Ron** sufficient dough To give us 〔**hope**〕 he'll pack his things and go.
esperar	*to wait (for), expect, hope (for)*	**Yes, spare ar**tless tax evaders Who 〔**wait**〕 in vain 〔**for**〕 Nader's Raiders.
esposo	*husband*	Yes, **Poe so** often voiced his woe in verse My 〔**husband**〕 thought him haunted by a curse.
estallar	*to burst, explode*	**Les, Thai yar**ns you have for hours rehearsed; Now tell us how your own life's bubble 〔**burst**〕.
estar	*to taste, be,*	I like to see **Tess star** in making jelly. It 〔**tastes**〕 like heaven and delights my belly.
estilo	*style, custom*	Yes, **tea (lo**w-calorie) is the 〔**style**〕 for drinking. You must adopt it if you're bent on shrinking.
estudiar	*to study*	**Bess, too, the ar**gument repeated: You 〔**study**〕 best when you are seated.

exigir	*to demand, insist*	He stocks a novel kind of beer.
		Demand some for Al**exey here**.

éxito	*success*	See R**ex eat o**ld meat from the leftover table.
		His fiscal success must be only a fable.

extranjero	*foreigner, stranger*	**Next, Ron Hare, ro**mantic foreigner ,
		Found a corpse and called the coroner.

Spanish	English	
fácil	*easy*	Do re mi **fa—sea l**ife is easy ,
		And hornpipes cheer us when we're queasy.
fe (f.)	*faith*	My faith in you is **fa**ding fast.
		Love was so good. Why can't it last?
fecha	*date (calendar)*	On this date a year ago,
		Fay cha-chaed and broke her toe.
feliz	*happy*	I'm happy that the tree **fell eas**t.
		It killed an Oriental beast.
feo, -a	*ugly*	**Fay o**r woman, fair or ugly ,
		Love her if she fits you snugly.
fiar	*to guar- antee, sell on credit, trust*	When Du**ffy ar**gues loud and long,
		I guarantee that he'll be wrong.

fiel	*faithful, loyal*	The ⬚*faithful* Duffy, **el**egant and ⬚*loyal*, Defends the king on his ancestral soil.
figura	*figure, coun- tenance, mien, shape*	The ta**ffy goo Ra**mona often ate Enlarged her ⬚*figure* to a forty-eight.
fijar	*to fix*	When they ⬚*fix* a decent price for board, In a ji**ffy har**mony's restored.
fin (m.)	*end*	The lawyer's **fee, n**o doubt, seems modest in amount. But in the ⬚*end*, I fear, he'll wreck your bank account.
fingir	*to pretend*	They say a little ca**ffeine here** and there Helps you ⬚*pretend* you're not the worse for wear.
firmar	*to sign*	**Fear Mar**ty's eagerness ⬚*to sign* Too promptly on the dotted line.
fondo	*bottom, depth*	Her parents threw the **phone Do**lores got 'em Into the well and smashed it on the ⬚*bottom*.
frío, -a	*cold*	Let's **free o**ld Tom from this ⬚*cold* world. His day is done, his flag is furled.
fruta	*fruit*	If **ruta**baga gives you gas, Eat some ⬚*fruit* and it will pass.
fuego	*fire*	A long, rou**gh way go**es up the hill. But there's a ⬚*fire* in every still.
fuente (f.)	*spring, fountain, source*	To**fu, Wen, ta**kes time, but it's a ⬚*spring* Of inspiration to a kitchen king.

fuera	*outside,* *out*	Jef**f, wear a** coat. It's very cold ⟦ *outside* ⟧. Just spray it with a mild insecticide.
fuerza	*strength,* *force*	Jose**ph, 'ware Sa**mantha's racing weakness! —And yet she had the ⟦ *strength* ⟧ to win the Preakness.

Spanish	**English**	
ganar	*to earn,* *win*	He owns a bar**gain ar**t store where he labors And ⟦ *earns* ⟧ some extra income drawing sabers.
gastar	*to spend,* *waste*	You ⟦ *spent* ⟧ our savings on your walk. I'm almost ga**ga. Star**t to talk!
gente (f.)	*people*	O **hen, ta**ke care! Avoid mishaps. Don't lay your eggs in ⟦ *people* ⟧'s laps.
gentil	*gentle,* *generous,* *kind*	The ⟦ *gentle* ⟧ pea**hen Teal**e acquired Produced no eggs, so she was fired.
golpe (m.)	*blow*	My **goal: pay** off my college debts, Then strike a ⟦ *blow* ⟧ for injured vets.
gordo, -a	*fat*	Gre**gor, though** ⟦ *fat* ⟧, can woo and win. I love him whether fat or thin.
gota	*drop*	**Go, To**m, get a kitchen mop. On my floor you've spilled a ⟦ *drop* ⟧.

gozar	*to enjoy*	There **go Ser**geant Carr and both his wives. Their laughter shows all three ⟨*enjoy*⟩ their lives.
grado	*degree*	Last Mardi **Gras, though** mostly pleasing, It got to one ⟨*degree*⟩ from freezing.
grave	*serious, grave, sober*	In Mardi **Gras Ba**be may become delirious. She heckles people whom she thinks too ⟨*serious*⟩ .
gritar	*to shout, scream*	**Gree**t **Tar**zan climbing down the tree. Just ⟨*shout*⟩ and ⟨*scream*⟩ and so will he.
guerra	*war*	⟨*War*⟩ broke out when Mom would wear a Faded dress from the brown-ba**g era**.
guiar	*to guide*	Mag**gie, ar**dent but inept, ⟨*Guided*⟩ me to where she slept.
gustar	*to enjoy, like*	Of all the works of culinary art I most ⟨*enjoy*⟩ my Annabel's **goose tar**t.
gusto	*taste, pleasure*	The **goose to**ld Ann what Ann told Lee: "You'll never know the ⟨*taste*⟩ of me."

Spanish	*English*	
hablar	*to talk, speak*	You must have learned ⏢to talk⏢ in something like **a Blar**ney Castle, Where people think a compliment is better than a hassle.
hacer	*to make, do*	**Ah, Sar**ah ⏢*made*⏢ a lot of big mistakes. But kindly gentlemen have soothed her aches.
hacia	*toward*	Ya claim I try to **boss ya**! Sweetheart, say not so. I only push ya gently ⏢*toward*⏢ the place ya wanta g(
hallar	*to find, think*	Although the weeds grow quickly in this heat, You ⏢*'ll find*⏢ I keep m**y yar**d and garden neat.
hambre (f.)	*hunger*	T**om, bra**ve soul, though faint with ⏢*hunger*⏢, Roundly cursed the gossip-monger.
hasta	*until, all the way to*	The **pasta** sitting on my plate Was good ⏢*until*⏢ I overate.
he aquí	*here is*	Hurr**ay! A key** to fit that lock! And ⏢*here's*⏢ another for the clock.
hecho	*fact, deed; p.p. of hacer*	The ⏢*fact*⏢ is, **HO**ME is the spellin' Of one place We the People don't raise hell in.
helar	*to freeze*	It's quite **a lar**k, I found, to skate on ice, But if you ⏢*freeze*⏢ your toes it's not so nice.

herida	*wound*	Kay, **wreathe a** hero's brow with laurel; He got his │ *wound* │ in your last quarrel.
herir	*to hurt, wound*	**A rear**-end crash │ *hurt* │ Bandit Boris' legs, So now he just robs banks with other yeggs.
hermano	*brother*	The two little │ *brothers* │ just won't get dressed. They've got to learn that th**eir ma know**s best.
hermoso, -a	*beautiful*	That Scotch **air Moe so** often whistles Is │ *beautiful* │ like Highland thistles.
hervir	*to boil*	You must **tear beer** right off your shopping list. —I won't! You make me │ *boil* │ when you insist!
hielo	*ice*	**Yea, Lo**renzo, flattering words are nice, But I'm afraid you're skating on thin │ *ice* │.
hierro	*iron*	Say, men of │ *iron* │, why **ye air o**ld myths That no one's heard of since the ancient Scyths.
hijo	*son*	Be**e ho**lds stocks and bonds. They're in the bank. She has her │ *son* │'s big legacy to thank.
hilo	*thread*	Be **lo**quacious. Spin your │ *thread* │. Talk him down till the subject's dead.
hogar (m.)	*hearth, home*	**Oh, guar**d with pride your │ *hearth* │ and │ *home* │; But stay in Paris or in Rome.
hoja	*leaf, page*	**O, ho**t Mama! Turn your journal │ *leaf* │. Forget the │ *page* │ that tells your long-time grief.
hombre (m.)	*man*	Go h**ome, bra**ve fellow, slumber if you can. In battle you have proved yourself a │ *man* │.
hombro	*shoulder*	Bring h**ome bro**cade upon your │ *shoulder* │ (Or velvet, since it's getting colder).

| hora | *hour* | Give me an | *hour* |, **or a** moment at least,
 And try not to roar like a ravening beast. |

hora   *hour*   Give me an | *hour* |, **or a** moment at least,
And try not to roar like a ravening beast.

hoy   *today*   Enj**oy** | *today* |. Regrets don't pay!
As for tomorrow—who's to say?

huerta   *garden,*   Catch those rogues—and I'll grant them pardon—
     orchard   Who **wear To**dd's boots when they weed their
     | *garden* | .

hueso   *bone*   Don't throw a**way so** many scraps,
But scrape the | *bones* | to bait our traps.

huevo   *egg*   We test Bo's buttermilk, **weigh Bo**'s | *eggs* |,
Pour Bo's beer into airtight kegs.
And still Bo walks on wobbly legs.

huir   *to flee*   We watched the witch d**o eer**ie dances,
But | *fled* | at last her ardent glances.

humano,   *human*   Look y**ou, Ma, no** | *human* | mind can know
-a   Where stars are born or clouds and comets go.

húmedo,   *humid*   I chose a **room, May, though** I knew
-a   This | *humid* | flat's too small for two.

humo   *smoke,*   **You, Moe**, sneered at that forlorn old bloke.
     vapor   Now his dreams have all gone up in | *smoke* | .

hundir   *to sink,*   **Soon dir**igibles filled the air;
     crush   They | *sank* | some U-boats cruising there.

Spanish	*English*	
idea	*idea*	The staff? **See! They a**dore their young employer. Ideas flow from factory to foyer.
ingenio	*genius*	**Dean Henny o**wns his genius can't explain Why he writes music only in the rain.
inventar	*to invent*	We don't este**em Ben, Tar**tar to the marrow, For he invented death by poisoned arrow.
ir	*to go*	The words you lavish on my brother Go in one **ear** and out the other.
ira	*wrath*	O sixties, **era** fraught with righteous wrath , 'Twas you that taught me manners, mirth, and math.
jamás	*never*	**Ha! Ma s**at down in the chief's own chair. We'd never expected to see her there.
jefe (m.)	*chief,* *boss*	**Hey, Fe**licia, call the chief . He'll put handcuffs on this thief.
joven	*young*	**Ho! Ben**, cut your capers. While we're young The wine of life is sweet upon the tongue.
juego	*game*	Curds and **whey go** well with childish games . But Muffet can't compete with older dames.

juez (m.)	*judge*	The guy **who ace**d this test with notes from Sonny Is now a $\boxed{\textit{judge}}$ and making lots of money.
jugar	*to play*	Girls **who gar**den $\boxed{\textit{play}}$ with fate: In middle years they vegetate.
juicio	*trial, judgment*	**Whee! See o**ld Judge Tort, so full of guile, At last, with all his cronies, brought to $\boxed{\textit{trial}}$.
junto, -a	*together*	Cal**houn to**ld Sandy, "Now we're here $\boxed{\textit{together}}$, Why don't we all go rolling in the heather?"
jurar	*to swear*	"**Hoorrah!" R**oberta cried, "I $\boxed{\textit{swear}}$ I found the body. I was there."
justo, -a	*correct, exact*	**Who sto**le Aaron's car? Some girl he necked? —I fear your supposition is $\boxed{\textit{correct}}$.
juventud (f.)	*youth*	**Who, Ben, to th**e call of $\boxed{\textit{youth}}$ responded? —Only I. The others all absconded.
juzgar	*to judge*	**Who's Gar**finkle $\boxed{\textit{to judge}}$ that I am lewd? He posed for sidewalk artists in the nude!

Spanish	English	
lago	*lake*	Oo la **la! Go** jump in the $\boxed{\textit{lake}}$. You're not from Paris. You're just a fake!

lana	*wool*	Is it a ram or is it a bull? **Lana** will know when she shears the	wool	.
lanzar	*to hurl,* *throw*	**Lon, Sar**tre	hurled	the javelin of thought Against a world halfway to madness wrought.
largo, -a	*long*	Key **Largo** is an island	long	and sultry, A perfect place in which to flaunt adultery.
leer	*to read*	The clergy complain that **lay er**rors besmirch Reports we	have read	on our good Mother Church.
lejos	*far*	Let's **lay Jos**é where he can rest at last, And,	far	from home, know all his troubles past.
letra	*letter (of* *alphabet),* *handwriting*	The p**late Ra**mona tossed into the flames Once bore the painted	letters	of our names.
ley (f.)	*law*	**Lay** down the	law	, sir, as you please, But no one tells me when to sneeze.
libra	*pound*	Sara **Lee brou**ght home a	pound	of butter When what we needed was a paper cutter.
libre	*free*	**Lee, bra**ve men like you, if right or wrong, Have helped to keep our country	free	and strong.
libro	*book*	**Lee bro**ke every rule in the	book	. None of us guessed he was really a crook.
ligero, -a	*light*	**Lee, hay ro**settes are fine to hang on Papa's horses, But just a	light	corsage for me is what our code endorses.
lista	*list, strip,* *stripe*	At **least a** dozen names were on the	list	: The girls at school who never have been kissed.

loco, -a	*insane, mad*	This **loco**motive seems to be │ *insane* │, Snorting and snarling like a bull in pain.
locura	*madness*	It's │ *madness* │ how you waste your time exploring Aristotle When our **low Cura**çao means you've got to buy a bottle.
lucha	*fight*	**Lou cho**ps up his meat so small He doesn't need to chew at all. But just involve him in a │ *fight* │, You'll find the chap knows how to bite.
luchar	*to struggle, fight*	**Lou char**red the steak, and how we hate it! We had │ *to struggle* │, but we ate it.
luego	*then*	In life the midd**le way go**es smooth and straight, │ *Then* │ brings us safely to the pearly gate.
lugar (m.)	*place*	**Lou, guar**d your priceless store of antique lace. Please don't begrime it in this sordid │ *place* │.
luz (f.)	*light*	Though **loose** connections dimmed the │ *light* │, Our passion glowed throughout the night.
llamar	*to call*	Chuck will tell **ya mar**velous old stories. │ *Call* │ him in to paint our former glories.
llanto	*crying*	Friend, **yon To**ledo blade you're eyeing Could slit your throat and end your │ *crying* │.
llegar	*to arrive*	**Yea, gar**dens are the places of the Lord, And yet, when we │ *arrive* │, we're rather bored.
llenar	*to fill*	You ghoul—**yea, nar**k—you work for the police. It's true you │ *fill* │ our need to keep the peace.

lleno, -a	*full*	The judge said, "**Yea, no** way will this race count! The jockeys are too ⌐ *full* ¬ of booze to mount."
llevar	*to carry, take, wear, transport*	**Yea, bar** the gate, and ⌐ *carry* ¬ in the wine. They stay forever who come here to dine.

Spanish	English	
maestro	*teacher, master*	The ⌐ *teacher* ¬ says my spurt in height'll Show Ma**ma estro**gens are vital.
mal	*badly*	**Ma'll** be ⌐ *badly* ¬ hurt to see Her daughter lose the spelling bee.
mandar	*to command, govern, order, send*	Sher**man, Dar**win taught us how we all survive. Nature's law ⌐ *commands* ¬: Stay fit, and stay alive.
manera	*way, manner*	"In some ⌐ *ways* ¬ guys I know," said Sarah, "Don't quite belong in the hu**man era.**"
mano (f.)	*hand*	**Ma, no** one but you will understand The need I sometimes feel to hold your ⌐ *hand* ¬.
manto	*cloak, mantle*	A rare Ver**mont to**rnado tore his ⌐ *cloak* ¬, But Nemo stood as steadfast as an oak.
mañana	*morning, tomorrow*	Hoot, **mon! Yan a**rises frisky: Every ⌐ *morning* ¬ he drinks whiskey.

mar (m.)	*sea*	Don't **mar** the ⟨ sea ⟩ with toxic waste. You'll kill the fish or spoil the taste.
más	*more*	**Ma s**teers the boat. I wonder where we're going. The ⟨ more ⟩ I ask, the more she just looks knowing.
mascar	*to chew*	**Ma scar**red her costly lower plate By ⟨ chewing ⟩ hard on what she ate.
matar	*to kill*	Der**mot, are** you talking sense? You ⟨ killed ⟩ that mouse in self-defense?
mayor	*larger,* *greater*	**My Yor**k's a busy English city, Fast growing ⟨ larger ⟩, more's the pity.
medida	*size,* *measure,* *measure-* *ment*	**May thee the** gods protect from heaven And keep your ⟨ size ⟩ at six or seven.
medio, -a	*half*	Deep dis**may the o**ld-time army hit Because its ancient, ⟨ half ⟩-wit general quit.
mejor	*better*	**May hoar**ds her pennies, says she likes it ⟨ better ⟩ Than being, like the average girl, a debtor.
menos	*less*	Dick considers **May no s**illy fool. She's ⟨ less ⟩ than eager, though, to go to school.
mente (f.)	*mind*	**Men ta**ke little time to shave and dress. The bathroom, like their ⟨ minds ⟩, stays in a mess!
mentir	*to lie*	**Men, tear**s and groans are out of place. Besides, you ⟨ 're lying ⟩ to my face.
mentira	*lie*	Your com**ment irri**tates my wife no end: She does tell ⟨ lies ⟩, but never to a friend.

merecer	*to deserve*	See **May race Er**rol to the kitchen sink. They've talked so much they both ⟨ **deserve** ⟩ a drink.
mes (m.)	*month*	Once a ⟨ **month** ⟩ I purchase **mace** To spray my neighbor's lecherous face.
metro	*subway*	The ⟨ **subway** ⟩'s where I met my **mate**. **Ro**mance began at Lake and State.
mezclar	*to mix*	In human strife Clark Kent ⟨ **will mix** ⟩, But *this* **mess Clar**k can't hope to fix.
miel (f.)	*honey*	Your lecture helped **me el**evate my thinking. But our supply of bread and ⟨ **honey** ⟩'s shrinking.
mientras	*while*	⟨ **While** ⟩ Nemo sat in the gloo**my entres**ol Some rats appeared, ignoring protocol.
mil	*thousand*	A ⟨ **thousand** ⟩ hot dogs at a **meal**! —For elephants it's no big deal.
mío, -a	*of mine, mine*	Oh **me, oh** my! What makes you whine and cry? —That girl ⟨ **of mine** ⟩ is dating another guy.
mirar	*to watch, look at*	⟨ **Watch** ⟩ **mere ar**tists change the way we think. It happens even when their paintings stink.
misa	*Mass*	To **me Sa**mantha seems to be a lass Who stops for whiskey on her way to ⟨ **Mass** ⟩.
mismo, -a	*same*	My friend, let's you and **me smo**ke one last pipe together, And then I'll plunge into the ⟨ **same** ⟩ old stormy weather.
modo	*way*	**Moe, though** bashful, got his foolish ⟨ **way** ⟩, For every dog has got to have his day.

moneda	*money, change, coin*	**Monet, the** famous artist, so they say, Made stacks of $\boxed{\text{money}}$ merely painting hay.
montaña	*mountain*	A deep **moan Tanya** uttered, turning blue, Then stammered, "Get me quick some $\boxed{\text{Mountain}}$ Dew!"
morir	*to die*	If you just gobble one **more ear** of corn You $\boxed{\text{'ll die}}$, or wish you never had been born.
mozo	*waiter, boy*	**Moe so** resented the flies in his stew That he called on the $\boxed{\text{waiter}}$ to swallow a few.
mucho, -a	*much*	I hope a **moo cho**kes all your cattle. $\boxed{\text{Much}}$ lowing makes my brains just rattle.
mudo, -a	*mute, silent*	S**mooth o**ld quarrels with your flute And end each fight by staying $\boxed{\text{mute}}$.
muestra	*sign, sample*	"You ought to take To**m west,**" **Ra**món suggested. "I see no $\boxed{\text{sign}}$ his mettle has been tested."
mujer (f.)	*woman*	A cow's **moo her**alds the break of day. Where's the $\boxed{\text{woman}}$ who feeds it hay?
mundo	*earth, world*	Look at the **moon. Do**n't ask me why It follows the $\boxed{\text{earth}}$ around the sky.
muy	*very*	Basco**m, we** too $\boxed{\text{very}}$ strongly hope You can persuade our children to elope.

Spanish	*English*	
nacer	*to be born*	The fur**nace Sar**ah stoked each morn Blew up the day her child $\boxed{\textit{was born}}$.
nada	*nothing*	**Nah, the** girl means $\boxed{\textit{nothing}}$ to me really. Besides, I find her all too squat and squeally.
nadie	*no one*	**Nah! The a**pes in zoos won't bite your finger. In fact, they grieve when $\boxed{\textit{no one}}$ wants to linger.
negar	*to refuse, deny*	**Nay, gar**bage shouldn't go to waste, So $\boxed{\textit{do}}$ n't $\boxed{\textit{refuse}}$ a tiny taste.
negro, -a	*black*	**Nay, grow** Mexican beans no more: I just threw up on the $\boxed{\textit{black}}$ tile floor.
nervioso, -a	*nervous*	**Ne'er be oh! so** tense and $\boxed{\textit{nervous}}$. You only face your wedding service.
ni . . . ni	*neither . . . nor*	K**nee** to k**nee** we used to say a prayer. But now I fear you $\boxed{\textit{neither}}$ know $\boxed{\textit{nor}}$ care.
nieto	*grandson*	Whit**ney ate o**ld crusts of bread. "My $\boxed{\textit{grandson}}$'s starving me," he said.
niño	*boy*	Na**neen, Yo**landa jumped with joy and shock When that new $\boxed{\textit{boy}}$ moved into the next block.

noche (f.)   *night*   Of late, those **no-cha**fe pants are all the rage
With girls who prance at ⟨ *night* ⟩ upon the
stage.

nombre
(m.)   *name*   To **Nome? Bra**ve fellow! Tell me, what's your
⟨ *name* ⟩?
—Nemo, or Nobody: It's all the same.

notar   *to note*   ⟨ *Will* ⟩ all please ⟨ *note* ⟩: This fag contains
no tar.
It tastes and smokes just like a fine cigar.

noticias   *news*   If there's no ⟨ *news* ⟩, if there's **no tea**,
See Oscar. He'll refund your fee.

novela   *novel*   **No bail? Ah**, me. Go get my English grammar.
I'll have to write my ⟨ *novel* ⟩ in the slammer.

novio   *boyfriend*   My ⟨ *boyfriend* ⟩ suffers **no B.O.**
His breath is bad from smoking, though.

nuevo, -a   *new,
different*   The strange ⟨ *new* ⟩ **way Bo** serves at tennis
Has no appeal; he's just a menace.

nunca   *never*   At **noon Ka**tinka ⟨ *never* ⟩ ate a bite,
But she came home at five and gorged all
night.

Spanish	English

obispo   *bishop*   **Obese po**licemen getting tighter
Made the | ***bishop*** | drop his miter.

objeto   *object*   **Job, hate o**ld Hilda if you feel you must.
At least you're not an | ***object*** | of her lust.

obra   *work,*   Inside my studio a c**obra** lurks,
work of   Coiling about my best and latest | ***works*** |.
art

ocultar   *to hide,*   B**o, cool tar**ts before you eat them.
conceal | ***Hide*** | them from the girls; then treat them.

odio   *hate*   **Jo**e, **the o**ld campaigner, insisted loud and long,
"Heap your | ***hate*** | upon the foe. The foe is
always wrong."

oficio   *trade*   To pay n**o fee, see o**ld man Glade.
Avoiding taxes is his | ***trade*** |.

oír   *to hear*   **O ear**s, you | ***hear*** | her tender sigh;
O eyes, you see she's less than shy.
So who can love her more than I?

ojo   *eye*   What will you say when the cops come by?
—Y**o ho** ho and mud in your | ***eye*** |!

ola   *wave*   Bob st**ole a** wigwam from a brave.
Were he a fish he'd steal a | ***wave*** |.

olvidar	*to forget*	**Colby, thar** she blows. But don't $\boxed{\textit{forget}}$ A killer whale will never make a pet.
olvido	*forget-fulness, oversight*	**Droll Bee, though** once a stunning stage success, Is troubled these days by $\boxed{\textit{forgetfulness}}$.
oprimir	*to press, oppress*	Why $\boxed{\textit{press}}$ me for the meaning of "pre-war"? You surely kn**ow "pre" mere**ly means "before."
orden (f.)	*com-mand, order*	**For the n**once I'm playing in the sand, But I'll come running back at your $\boxed{\textit{command}}$.
oro	*gold*	**Oh, ro**mantic dreams of love and $\boxed{\textit{gold}}$! They vanish swiftly as a tale that's told.
osar	*to dare*	**Oh, sar**casm will never make me yield. I $\boxed{\textit{'ll dare}}$ to prove it on the battlefield.
otro, -a	*other, another*	The **coat Ro**berto chanced to purchase at a sale Outlasted all his $\boxed{\textit{others}}$, for it's a coat of mail.

P

Spanish	*English*	
pagar	*to pay*	**Pa, Gar**finkel $\boxed{\textit{pays}}$ all his doctor bills But just won't take those nasty headache pills.
país (m.)	*country (father-land)*	**Pa, Eas**ter eggs now cost a buck, or near it. The $\boxed{\textit{country}}$ must be full of Easter spirit.

palo	*stick, cane*	**Pa, lo**w rates will end at ten precisely, So get your hat and ⬚ *stick* , both polished nicely.
pan (m.)	*bread*	The **pon**tiff brought our group a loaf of ⬚ *bread* . "My own infallible recipe," he said.
papel (m.)	*paper*	**Pa pel**ted Ma with old fly ⬚ *paper* When she confessed her latest caper.
para	*in order to, for*	**Pa ro**bbed little Ernie's piggy bank ⬚ *In order to* pursue some silly prank.
parar	*to stop*	Cas**par, are** you now a traffic cop? I fear you've learned to go, but not ⬚ *to stop* .
parecer	*to seem, appear*	See **Pa race Sar**ah! Now he's caught her: It ⬚ *seems* he's horrified his daughter.
partir	*to rend, crack, split*	Cas**par, tear**s and pleas are all in vain. You ⬚ *rend* my heart but cannot end the pain.
pasar	*to happen, pass*	"What ⬚ *happened* , Pa**pa," Ser**geant Poe demanded, "To all those daring men you once commanded?"
paso	*step*	A ⬚ *step* a s**pa so** rich can well afford Would be to give us wine with bed and board.
paz (f.)	*peace*	The press has just issued his **pos**thumous work. ⬚ *Peace* to his bones! (He was really a jerk.)
pecado	*sin*	A voice divine that soared above the din **Spake ah! tho**se words that freed my heart from ⬚ *sin* .
pecho	*chest, breast*	The guard I **pay cho**se not to do his best. He did own up, to get it off his ⬚ *chest* .

pedir	*to ask, ask for, request*	**Pay th' eer**ie creature half a dollar, But ⌐ask⌐ him bluntly not to holler.
peligro	*danger*	I'll **pay Lee gro**ss sums to keep this stranger From putting me and those I love in ⌐danger⌐.
pelo	*hair*	You **pay low** prices for your ⌐hair⌐, And that is why the people stare.
pena	*pain, sorrow, suffering*	In S**pain a**person learns to suffer. His ⌐pain⌐ will only make him tougher.
pensar	*to think*	I ⌐think⌐ a lecture on Old Irish art Will surely o**pen Sar**ge O'Brien's heart.
perder	*to lose*	**Pare their** ripe fruit, but leave my apple whole. Who scorns the skin ⌐has lost⌐ the apple's soul.
perezoso, -a	*lazy*	**Pare a so-so** fruit, and you may find ⌐Lazy⌐ insects have already dined.
pero	*but*	Put him on the **payro**ll, ⌐but⌐ Don't forget the guy's a nut.
perro	*dog*	We saw two figures struggling through the fog. The **pair o**'ertook us—Buster and his ⌐dog⌐.
pesar	*to weigh*	**Pay Ser**geant Nash ⌐to weigh⌐ the odds. We'll leave our fate to unknown gods.
peso	*weight*	You **pay so** well your models put on ⌐weight⌐, So no one ever asks them for a date.
pez (m.)	*fish (in water)*	**Pay s**ome guard to get me out! —Poor ⌐fish⌐, you just ain't got no clout.
picar	*to prick, sting*	The hap**py car**load, munching Fritos, ⌐Were pricked⌐ each moment by mosquitoes.

pie (m.)	*foot*	Snoo**py A**da spied once more— Caught her **foot** in my back door.
piel (f.)	*skin*	Unhap**py el**ders everywhere I've been Have seen how I get under people's **skin** .
pierna	*leg*	**Pierre kno**cked out for once his hated rival. I'd bet a **leg** against his own survival.
pieza	*room*	The Ho**pi ace** arrived. He filled the **room** With looks of mingled glamor, guts, and gloom.
pintura	*picture,* *painting*	Let the spal**peen tour a** foreign city. He's sure to bring back **pictures** less than pretty.
placer	*to please*	We **were** not **pleased** , but stood amazed To see the hoo**pla Sar**ah raised.
pleno, -a	*full*	Natasha's **play No**bel has quite ignored. The **full** truth is, it left the judges bored.
pobre	*poor*	The gallant **Poe bra**ved icy wind and weather So he and **poor** Lenore could be together.
pobreza	*poverty*	Bep**po, brace a** fence post here and there. Conceal a **poverty** so raw and bare.
poco, -a	*little (in* *quantity)*	Phil tried to **poke o**ld Herman in the eye. He whined a **little** and began to cry.
poder	*can, to be* *able*	The foul Gesta**po—there**'s an aberration That shocked the world and **could** have wrecked a nation.
polvo	*dust*	**Poll Bo**'s playmates. Can they if they must First wield a tomahawk, then bite the **dust** ?
poner	*to set,* *place*	Corn **pone ne'er** requires a label. Just **set** it steaming on the table.

| por | *along* | **Pour** the beer ⎡ *along* ⎤ the pier.
 The girls will find you, never fear. |

| por | *through* | **Pour** the cognac ⎡ *through* ⎤ my fingers.
 Half the day the fragrance lingers. |

| por qué | *why* | **Pork a**bly roasted makes your dinner easy.
 —⎡ **Why** ⎤ don't you serve it often?—It's too greasy. |

| porvenir (m.) | *future* | It's New Year's. **Pour Ben ir**idescent wine
 And toast the ⎡ *future* ⎤ and the Auld Lang Syne. |

| poseer | *to possess* | Did **Poe say er**rant knights and royalty are needed?
 —No, joy ⎡ *possessed* ⎤ him when he learned a king seceded. |

| preciso, -a | *necessary, concise, exact, precise* | **Pray see so** many lovely things in Rome
 It won't be ⎡ *necessary* ⎤ to come home. |

| predicar | *to preach* | Just **pray the car** has power enough to reach
 That Promised Land of which you love ⎡ *to preach* ⎤. |

| pregunta | *question* | **Pray, goon, ta**boos will save your skin from these indignant people
 Who wish, no ⎡ *question* ⎤, you may hang from some convenient steeple. |

| preguntar | *to ask (a question), inquire* | **Pray, goon, tar** and feather the lawless league.
 ⎡ **Ask** ⎤ them when they'll end their dark intrigue. |

| premio | *reward, prize* | O priest, just **pray me o**ver this last financial hurdle.
 And here is your fit ⎡ *reward* ⎤ —a beautiful purloined girdle. |

prender	*to take, fasten, seize*	Po**p, rend air**, and if you must, say charms, But [**take**] your errant daughter in your arms.
preso, -a	*in jail; person apprehended*	I **pray so** hard I wring my hands and wail. And yet somehow I always land [**in jail**].
prestar	*to lend, loan*	For the last time, **press Tar**zan's hand. You [**lent**] him money? Let it stand.
prevenir	*to prepare, warn*	**Pray, Ben, ir**rigate your far-flung fields, And then [**prepare**] your men for bounteous yields.
primo, -a	*cousin*	The **pre-Mo**saic world is steeped in mystery. At least that's what my [**cousin**] learned in history.
prisa	*haste*	'Twas just a ca**price, a** moment's whim, Conceived in [**haste**], pursued with vim.
privar	*to deprive*	A Ca**pri bar** [**deprived**] me of my cash, Yet I admit it was a heavenly bash.
probar	*to test, probe, prove, try*	**Probe ar**my captains, [**test**] them as you will. Esprit de corps will keep the scoundrels still.
pronto	*soon, prompt, quickly, ready*	My friends who went to buy some peanut butter [**Soon**] found me **prone, toe** broken, in the gutter.
propio, -a	*own*	"I'm **pro-P.O.**," said desperate Joan, "With P for Property, O for [**Own**]."
proseguir	*to proceed, continue*	You're a **pro, say gear** and garments. If you [**proceed**] you'll catch the varmints.

prueba	*proof*	**Prue, Abe a**ssured me he had $\boxed{\textit{proof}}$ You dated some big-city goof.
pueblo	*town*	**Pooh! Abe lo**ads trucks in $\boxed{\textit{town}}$. His muscle Assures he'll win in every tussle.
puerta	*door*	Why do you let Po**p wear Ta**hiti sandals? You've opened up the $\boxed{\textit{door}}$ to endless scandals.
puerto	*port,* *harbor*	They made Po**p wear to**bacco-colored shorts While chasing after spies in foreign $\boxed{\textit{ports}}$.
punto	*point*	When Ben's har**poon to**re up the joint I guess the owner got the $\boxed{\textit{point}}$.

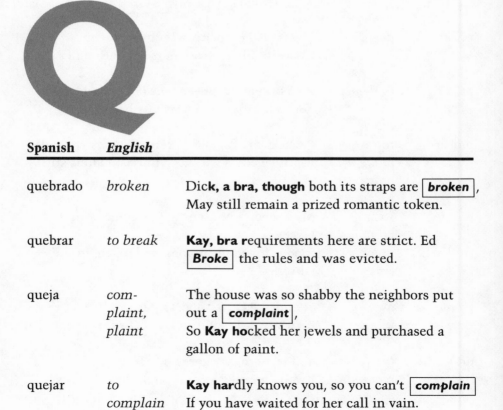

Spanish	*English*	
quebrado	*broken*	Dic**k, a bra, though** both its straps are $\boxed{\textit{broken}}$, May still remain a prized romantic token.
quebrar	*to break*	**Kay, bra r**equirements here are strict. Ed $\boxed{\textit{Broke}}$ the rules and was evicted.
queja	*com-* *plaint,* *plaint*	The house was so shabby the neighbors put out a $\boxed{\textit{complaint}}$, So **Kay ho**cked her jewels and purchased a gallon of paint.
quejar	*to* *complain*	**Kay har**dly knows you, so you can't $\boxed{\textit{complain}}$ If you have waited for her call in vain.

quemar	*to burn*	**Kay mar**veled first and then made haste to burn The letter that implored her to return.

querer	*to like,* *love,* *want,* *wish*	**Kay rare**ly likes a bookish guy, But you can win her if you try.

querido, -a	*beloved,* *dear*	**Kay, wreathe o**r hang fresh blossoms on his bier. Then turn, for your beloved is not here.

queso	*cheese*	O**K, so** you devoured the cheese. Now down the milk, your wife decrees.

quitar	*to leave*	Jane left the house in wrath, to use no more The house **key Tar**zan kept above the door.

Spanish	English

raíz (f.)	*root*	My**ra, Eas**t and West have stained our boots. At last we've found a place to put down roots.

rama	*branch*	**Drama** struck the Hi-Lo Ranch When Fred was felled by an oak-tree branch.

ramo	*sprig,* *small* *branch,* *spray*	The **prom o'**ershadows every other show As Christmas trees do sprigs of mistletoe.

rasgo	*feature, trait*	I warn you, **Ross, go** over every feature Before you sign a contract with this creature.
rato	*while, moment*	A sylvan **grotto** held me for a while , But soon I couldn't live without your smile.
raza	*breed, lineage, race*	The alba**ross a**ppalled the silly seaman As if the breed were fathered by a demon.
real	*royal*	**Pray Ol**iver to seek the royal favor So he can face the court without a quaver.
reclamar	*to claim, demand (trans.), complain (intrans.)*	Pa, **rake La Mar** across the coals: He claims to win each time he bowls.
recoger	*to collect, gather, pick up*	**Ray, coher**ence is the thing you lack. Collect your thoughts and hurl the insults back.
recorrer	*to go through, traverse*	**Rake, or air** at least, this musty hay. Go through the barn and throw the trash away.
recto, -a	*straight*	Mama w**recked o**ld Oliver's Chevrolet. The road was straight but he wouldn't get out of her way.
recuerdo	*memory, remembrance*	Don't let D**rake wear tho**se funny underclothes That leave a memory where'er he goes.
regla	*rule*	**G**reg, **La** Verne is breaking every rule . —You learn to do that when you go to school.
regresar	*to regress, return*	**Ray, gray ser**geant, sadly I confess Your mind is gone; you're starting to regress .

reina	*queen*	Only the hungry and the lean Throughout her **reign o**pposed the	queen	.
reír	*to laugh*	**Ray ir**ritates the guys with whom he's working Because he	laughs	when they declare he's shirking.
renta	*rent,* *income,* *revenue*	B**rent, a**ppalled by soaring	rent	, Hocked his car and bought a tent.
reponer	*to restore,* *replace*	**Rape? Oh, ne'er** this isle is soiled by crime. Peace	has restored	the olden, golden time.
requerir	*to need,* *require*	**Ray, Kay rear**ed your less than splendid brood. Now she herself	needs	your solicitude.
revolver	*to mix,* *stir, turn* *over*	**Ray, bowl bare**, but never	mix	 This sport with other kinds of kicks.
rey (m.)	*king*	A **ray** of hope lights up the gloom: The	king	has rented our front room.
rezar	*to pray*	X-**ray Ser**geant Ashly's wounded back And	pray	he doesn't know he's got the sack.
ribera	*bank,* *shore*	I see an ang**ry bear u**pon the	bank	. Shall we advance upon him with our tank? (Or is it merely something that I drank?)
río	*river*	C**reo**le food's too full of spice. I've thrown my lunch in the	river	twice.
risa	*laugh,* *laughter*	Ma**rie so**bbed hard. The foolish girl supposes That life is just a bowl of	laughs	and roses.
robar	*to rob*	You must p**robe Ar**thur's links with crime. He	robbed	his Ma of her last dime.

roca	*rock*	The **crow ca**vorted on some $\boxed{\textit{rocks}}$ With Mama's bra and Dad's old socks.
rodear	*to surround, encircle*	**Row they ar**tfully or like beginners, They $\boxed{\textit{'ll}}$ soon $\boxed{\textit{surround}}$ our boat and seize our dinners.
rogar	*to pray, beg, plead*	That **rogue Ar**thur snatched away my purse! Come back, I $\boxed{\textit{pray}}$, or dread your mother's curse!
rojo, -a	*red*	Mon**roe, ho**ld on. It's just as I said. The students have painted the whole town $\boxed{\textit{red}}$.
romper	*to break*	**Rome per**ished when its leaders got the itch $\boxed{\textit{To break}}$ their country's laws and then get rich.
ropa	*clothing, clothes*	I'll **rope a** cow for leather $\boxed{\textit{clothing}}$ — A job that fills my heart with loathing.
rostro	*face, coun- tenance, visage*	I'll feed your $\boxed{\textit{face}}$ with something really yummy: A **roast ro**bust enough to fill your tummy.
rumbo	*direction, course*	The **room Bo** chose was in a humble section. He settled there to find a new $\boxed{\textit{direction}}$.

S

Spanish	English	
saber	*to know (facts)*	Li**sa, bur**y false or useless knowledge, Including some I know you got in college.
sabio, -a	*wise*	Your song's too **sobby. Oh**, 'twere wise to sing Of youth and love and all that sort of thing.
sacar	*to take out*	**Sock Ar**thur, tie him up the way we planned, And take out all the cash he has on hand.
sal (f.)	*salt, grace, wit, humor*	Below the salt **Sol** made her sit, Ignoring all her grace and wit .
salsa	*gravy, sauce*	Lieutenant **Sol sa**luted Colonel Davy: "Sir, may I ask you how you made that gravy ?"
salto	*leap*	**Sol to**ld all your friends you've made the leap To this year's Cadillac from last year's Jeep.
salvar	*to save*	**Sol bar**red the doorway leading to the kitchen. Ma saved us neatly when she started bitchin'.
sangre (f.)	*blood*	Pres**s on, gray** steed, you're going well. I knew you'd do it: Blood will tell.
santo, -a	*holy, saintly*	I think thi**s onto**logical research Is seldom carried on by Holy Church.
secar	*to dry*	**Say, Car**l, do arbitrate this wrangle. Good sense dries tears when in-laws tangle.

seco, -a	*dry*	On us, they **say, Co**lombians rely. You think we ought to leave them high and $\boxed{\textit{dry}}$?
seda	*silk*	They **say the** members of this cult Wear only $\boxed{\textit{silk}}$ when they're adult.
seguir	*to follow*	**Say ghee r**epels. It $\boxed{\textit{follows}}$, then, I say, You'll never fry your food the Indian way.
según	*according to*	**Say, goon,** $\boxed{\textit{according to}}$ the schools You're only good at breaking rules.
seguro, -a	*sure, certain, safe*	The girls **say goo ro**lled out the oven door. I'm $\boxed{\textit{sure}}$ we'll have to scrub the kitchen floor.
semana	*week*	The boys **say Ma kno**cked out a thug or two. Next $\boxed{\textit{week}}$ she may be practicing on you.
semejante	*like, similar*	**Say, May, Hahn ta**kes all your time and money. How can you let him call you names $\boxed{\textit{like}}$ Honey?
sencillo, -a	*simple*	Ben**sen, see Yo**landa smile. —True love?—Oh no, it's $\boxed{\textit{simple}}$ guile.
sentar	*to seat*	The general **sent ar**my troops to save us And barber chairs in which $\boxed{\textit{to seat}}$ and shave us.
sentir	*to feel, feel sorry*	The fallen leaves **sent tear**s to all our eyes. We $\boxed{\textit{feel}}$ the chill of death when summer dies.
serio, -a	*serious, sober*	You **say Rio**'s hardly a place to be $\boxed{\textit{serious}}$? —The carnival season is simply delirious.
servir	*to serve*	Fop**s air beer** in public places And $\boxed{\textit{serve}}$ their guests with foolish graces.
siempre	*always*	You should **see Em pray** daily at the shrine. When she gets home she $\boxed{\textit{always}}$ seems to shine.

siglo	*century*	I **see glo**be-circling planes take off each day And wish they were a ⬚ *century* away.
siguiente	*next,* *following*	We all can **see ghee enter**ing our culture. ⬚ *Next* year no doubt we'll feast on roasted vulture.
sin	*without*	Tom left May ⬚ *without* a bean. When he came home she made a **scene**.
sin embargo	*however,* *never-* *theless*	I think I've never **seen Em bar goa**tees. ⬚ *However*, I suspect they make her sneeze.
sino	*but*	I fear I **see no** virtues in her, ⬚ *but* Only the vices found in every slut.
sitio	*place*	You **see, tea o**nly finds a worthy ⬚ *place* Where socializing is an act of grace.
soberbio, -a	*arrogant*	He hates the smell of camp, and al**so bear B.O.** Since he's become so ⬚ *arrogant*, it's time for him to go.
sobre	*upon, on*	**So, bra**ve leader, sit alone ⬚ *Upon* your newly paid-for throne.
sol (m.)	*sun*	My **soul** is like a winter ⬚ *sun*. It sheds no glow on anyone.
soler	*to be ac-* *customed* *to*	Ben, as **sole heir** to his uncle's estate, ⬚ *Is accustomed to* having his choice of a date.
solo, -a	*alone*	She's **so lo**quacious when ⬚ *alone*, She even talks to the dial tone.
soltar	*to loosen,* *untie*	The shoe **sole Tar**zan once had thought so neat ⬚ *Was loosened* by the puddles on the street.

sonar	*to sound*	**So Nar**vik is the site of our next meeting. It ⟦ **sounds** ⟧ as if we'll get an Arctic greeting.
soñar	*to dream*	Pepys**' own yar**n describes how Britain fared When church and state together ⟦ **dreamed** ⟧ and dared.
sostener	*to maintain, support, sustain*	**So, stain Er**ic's record with a fiction? Such tricks will just ⟦ **maintain** ⟧ the present friction.
subir	*to climb, go up, mount*	**Sue, beer** won't help you ⟦ **climb** ⟧ that rugged peak. Rather, sip tea or water from the creek.
suceder	*to happen, follow, occur*	**Sue, say their** confections meet your taste: It still may ⟦ **happen** ⟧ that they go to *waist*.
sueldo	*salary*	My ⟦ **salary** ⟧ runs to a **swell do**nation, So here is a check for a homeless Haitian.
sueño	*dream*	The **swain yo**ked up his clumsy barnyard team And with his sweetheart drove into a ⟦ **dream** ⟧.
suerte (f.)	*luck*	I **swear ta**me pigs have all the ⟦ **luck** ⟧. They roll in mud and don't get stuck.
sujetar	*to subdue*	**Sue, hate Ar**thur if you can. You ⟦ **'ll** ⟧ not ⟦ **subdue** ⟧ this willful man.
sujeto	*person, subject*	What makes **Sue hate o**ld gentlemen so much? —Some ⟦ **person** ⟧ used to beat her with a crutch.
suma	*sum*	Always as**sume a** client isn't dumb Even if you see him suck his thumb. But do not lend him any major ⟦ **sum** ⟧.

suponer	*to suppose*	Your **soup? Oh, ne'er** I've supped on broth so tasty. —Your wife's, I must $\boxed{\textit{suppose}}$, is pale and pasty.
suspiro	*sigh*	Come on, **Sue, spear o**ld, hungry alligators. Just hear their $\boxed{\textit{sighs}}$! They think we're wildlife-haters.
susto	*fear*	**Sue sto**le almost everything I had Before the $\boxed{\textit{fear}}$ of vengeance drove her mad.

Spanish	*English*	
tabla	*tablet*	Eig**ht oblo**ng $\boxed{\textit{tablets}}$ waited in the room. Eight speakers grimly prophesied our doom.
tal	*such*	You broke our party into factions. We will not **tol**erate $\boxed{\textit{such}}$ actions!
tal vez	*perhaps*	This bust has lost its me**tal base**. $\boxed{\textit{Perhaps}}$ Some guest concealed it underneath his wraps.
también	*also, too*	**Tom, be an**ything you think you'll like, Just so you needn't $\boxed{\textit{also}}$ go on strike.
tampoco	*not either, neither, nor*	**Tom, poke o**ld Jim, and do not give the guy a breather. And if he asks for pardon, you should $\boxed{\textit{not}}$ grant that $\boxed{\textit{either}}$.

tapar	*to cover up, cover, stop up*	**Top ar**tists cover up a hoax? This must be one of your bad jokes.
tarde	*late (adv.), afternoon (f.)*	This movie s**tar, they** say, arises late , Then goes out looking for a breakfast date.
tela	*web, cloth, screen*	It's just a fairy **tale a** nanny told About a magic web that turned to gold.
temblar	*to shake, shiver, shudder, tremble*	Don'**t aim blar**ney at my dear old nanny. She '**ll shake** with laughter; she's both couth and canny.
temer	*to fear*	We'll all s**tay mer**ry while the fete continues. Though drink, I fear , is rotting out our sinews.
tender	*to stretch out, lay out, stretch*	Please **tend Er**ic as you did before: Just stretch the drunkard out and let him snore.
ternura	*tender-ness*	**Tear neura**sthenic moods from troubled Bess, And treat her firmly but with tenderness .
tienda	*store*	You should see Aun**tie end a** fight In Uncle's store on Saturday night.
tierno, -a	*tender*	Let our par**ty air no** rankling doubts. Tender topics lead to angry bouts.
tierra	*land*	A pi**ty Erro**l left (the jerk) So little land and so much work.
tío	*uncle*	I'm content with **tea o**r coffee Plus one small taste of Uncle 's toffee.

tirar	*to draw, pull, shoot*	**S**teer **Ar**thur to the fire, and all together We $\boxed{\textbf{'ll draw}}$ the curtains on the stormy weather.
tocar	*to play (a musical instrument), touch*	I met Joe Bar**tow car**ting home a banjo. I sneered and muttered, "$\boxed{\textit{\textbf{Play}}}$ it if you can, Joe."
todavía	*still, yet*	We have to **tow the Bea**trice to harbor And $\boxed{\textit{\textbf{still}}}$ get in a visit to the barber.
todo, -a	*every*	I'm sure the villain trod upon my **toe**, **Though** $\boxed{\textbf{every}}$ body swears it isn't so.
tomar	*to take*	Bere**ft, O Mar**garet, of your attentions, I'll have $\boxed{\textit{\textbf{to take}}}$ a chance on new inventions.
torpe	*stupid, clumsy, dull*	Jim **tore pay**ola from the $\boxed{\textit{\textbf{stupid}}}$ jerks Who batten on their customers and clerks.
torre (f.)	*tower*	My **toe! Ray** stepped on it every hour! I've hustled him back to his ivory $\boxed{\textit{\textbf{tower}}}$.
trabajar	*to work*	I dare no**t rob a har**dware store. I $\boxed{\textit{\textbf{'d}}}$ rather $\boxed{\textbf{work}}$ till stiff and sore.
traer	*to bring*	$\boxed{\textit{\textbf{Bring}}}$ **extra air**, inflate his ego. If you can't go, why not let me go?
trás (de)	*behind, after, beyond*	Tha**t ros**ter clearly shows the culprit's name. $\boxed{\textit{\textbf{Behind}}}$ that faltering script we sense his shame.
tratar	*to treat*	**Trot ar**tists out and let them $\boxed{\textit{\textbf{treat}}}$ of painting, At least until we're at the point of fainting.

trato	*trade,* *dealings,* *treatment*	I hope you ladies don't believe tha**t rot** **O**'Malley spilled about my trade in pot.
trazar	*to trace*	The Con**tra ser**geant couldn't trace That dark, elusive Indian face.
trigo	*wheat*	A **tree go**es "ssssh" in the warm spring breeze, And the wheat sways golden about my knees.
triste	*sad*	My Christmas **tree stay**ed green the whole year round, Because I left it growing in the ground. It's sad no better method could be found.
tropa	*troop*	I **trow Pa**tricia followed the army troop . 'Twas just last week her sergeant flew the coop.
trozo	*chunk,* *piece*	Sir Kay, you've come to fight the dragon? —I **trow so**, else I've got a jag on. —Then toss the brute this chunk of bread. He'll wolf it down and then drop dead.

Spanish	*English*	
único, -a	*only*	They're a **looney co**rps of lonely men Whose only wish is to marry again.
vacío, -a	*void,* *empty*	**Bah! See o**ld men around the park deployed. —Let them alone: Their lives are null and void .

valer	*to be worth*	With Kim**ball heir** to all his uncle's wealth It' s worth our while to win his heart by stealth.
valor (m.)	*value, worth*	Tu**bal or**ganized his prison time To learn the value scales of crime.
vaso	*(drinking) glass*	**Bah! so** often empty is your glass I fear you always let the bottle pass. —I had to give it up. It gives me gas.
vecino	*neighbor*	My neighbor , shocked by some **base scene or** story, Begins to crumple like a morning glory.
vejez (f.)	*old age*	The bomb **bay has**tily unlocked, its dreadful burden fell. Old age has taught me: Only man can send the world to hell.
vencer	*to defeat, conquer*	Tell **Ben cer**emony will defeat The friendly atmosphere we find so sweet.
vengar	*to avenge, revenge*	Look, **Ben, gar**goyles line the sacred dome. —Let's knock a nice one off and take it home. —They would avenge it quickly back in Rome.
venir	*to come*	The hounds **bay near** his grave each night. So come . Behold this touching rite.
ventura	*luck*	I had to help **Ben tour a** foreign city. By great good luck , I found him wise and witty.
ver	*to see*	Two scenes that I can't **bear** to see : Hans with you and Fritz with me.
verano	*summer*	**Bear** R**on no** grudge because he cheated. In summer he gets overheated.

verde	*green*	**Bare they** fought and bare they died, All scattered on the green hillside.
vergüenza	*shame*	**Bear goo, Ensig**n Smith with shame insists, Brings out pimples on his thighs and wrists.
vestido	*clothing, dress, suit*	Our **best tea, though** cheap and drunk with loathing, Must serve us still, just like our shabby clothing .
vestir	*to dress (trans.)*	**Bess, tear**s will get an actress nowhere fast, So dress your body and rejoin the cast.
vez (f.)	*time (in a series)*	I bet my last, my one thin dime, I'll get to **base** the second time .
viaje (m.)	*trip*	**Be ah! hay**-fever-free this trip . Just take some pills to stop the drip.
vicio	*vice*	Does timid Sister **Bee see o**ver her shoulder Visions of vice from tales her mother told her?
vida	*life*	O clown, this has to **be the** life you chose, Or else you wouldn't wear those silly clothes.
viejo, -a	*old*	Her old **B.A. (Ho**me Ec., I think) Got her a job at a kitchen sink.
viento	*wind*	**Be ento**mologist or priest or barber, The winds of fate will bring you safe to harbor.
vista	*view*	You **beast, a**way! Your figure blocks my view . Please give me more of it and less of you.
viudo	*widower*	**Be you, though** you're a widower , aware That lots of single women wait out there.

vivir	*to live*	You must **be Beer**y Joe's surviving kin. How can you ⟨ *live* ⟩ in such a den of sin?
vivo, -a	*living,* *alive*	**Bee, Bo**hemian as she seems to be, Is like a ⟨ *living* ⟩ iceberg when with me.
volar	*to fly*	A rain**bow lar**gely occupies the sky. The dazzled birds can find no room ⟨ *to fly* ⟩.
volver	*to return* *(intrans.)*	When Bo ⟨ *returns* ⟩, he will be told The Rose **Bowl bear**s his name in gold.
voz (f.)	*voice*	Reginald's ⟨ *voice* ⟩ is the family's **boast**; It pierces the night like the wail of a ghost.

Spanish	*English*	
yerno	*son-in-* *law*	My ⟨ *son-in-law* ⟩ is no great catch. His sill**y air no** man can match.
zapato	*shoe*	**Sop Otto**'s cocktail off his lap. Untie his ⟨ *shoes* ⟩ and let him nap.
zumo	*juice*	The folks **assume o**ld Hiram is obtuse. —Perhaps he's only heavy on the ⟨ *juice* ⟩.

Final Exam

HOW WELL HAVE you learned the Spanish words you have studied in this book? The following short test will answer this question.

Each of the 50 jingles below contains the sounds of a Spanish word that you have learned from this book, but the jingles themselves you have not seen before. The jingles are constructed just like those in the vocabulary section. The English word is boxed, but the Spanish word is not marked. See if you can find and underscore the consecutive syllables that approximate the sound of the Spanish word. (Remember that the boxed verb may appear in a form other than the infinitive.)

When you have finished the test, look up the English words in the glossary to see if you got the right answers. If your answers are all correct, you have a score of 100 and can congratulate yourself on a not inconsiderable achievement. If you got as many as 35 right you may consider that you passed with a score of 70 and are ready for a brief review.

1. Ma, say tame lions make you boil.
   Just stir them up with olive │ *oil* │.

2. Ah, Sue, caress this helpless bugger.
   He's just a pup who wants some │ *sugar* │.

3. Raquel, jump into │ *that* │ swimming pool.
   It's much too hot to go to school!

4. | **Here** | is a key for you and me.
   Keep it a secret until we're free.

5. Doll, go look for | **something** | strong and cold.
   Then wash the glasses out as you've been told.

6. Let Margaret court Arthur as she will,
   She's | **cut** | her chance of winning him to nil.

7. Ah, see your girlfriend make a fuss.
   How can you leave her despairing | **thus** | ?

8. Phoebe, end this yen to whine.
   Just shut your trap till you are | **fine** | .

9. Bob, a Chinese sage long since averred:
   "Confide your feelings only to a | **bird** | ."

10. Ah, Sue, luck failed you. But the skies are | **blue** | .
    The storm will pass, and next time so will you.

11. By large expenditures in France
    The clumsy fellow learned | **to dance** | .

12. An Inca posse, with some skilled instructions,
    Is | **capable** | of handling native ructions.

13. Sell your car, sell pot and pail.
    Then disappear—or go to | **jail** | .

14. The car Nate filled with rancid | **meat** |
    Blew up and dumped him in the street.

15. Your composition, stamped and sealed,
    Fell in a pond in yonder | **field** | .

16. Cohn sway Lorraine? I hardly think he can.
    She finds small | **consolation** | now in man.

17. A mini-crew sufficed to ferry us.
    Our ⟦ *cross* ⟧ proclaims we're not nefarious.

18. Dee a ⟦ *day* ⟧ in the meadow lay.
    She caught a fever that wasn't hay.

19. May lay here upon her bed
    And ⟦ *chose* ⟧ to think she'd soon be dead.

20. Les, coo charms in ladies' ears.
    They've learned ⟦ *to listen* ⟧ through the years.

21. My hen takes ⟦ *people* ⟧ into the barn,
    Cackling over some egghead yarn.

22. Pa, start up the motor, let's get zinging.
    We'll sail ⟦ *until* ⟧ we hear the mermaids singing.

23. A ⟦ *thread* ⟧ of common sense unites our nation:
    We guard our treasure in a key location.

24. "Aloha," whispers every ⟦ *leaf* ⟧ .
    It tells of love, it tells of grief.

25. Eat curds and whey. Go use the gym.
    Pursue each ⟦ *game* ⟧ with verve and vim.

26. You will not find Lon sorry for his crimes.
    He ⟦ *hurls* ⟧ the blame upon his life and times.

27. Lee brought home a ⟦ *pound* ⟧ of sale-priced liver.
    We ate it grimly, but without a quiver.

28. Her golden hair hangs long and loose.
    It holds the ⟦ *light* ⟧ like orange juice.

29. Some men tyrannize and some men cringe.
    I cannot ⟦ *lie* ⟧ : Your husband's on the fringe.

30. For plowing, Don yokes man and beast together,
    But both will suffer $\boxed{\textit{damage}}$ in hot weather.

31. Moe, though courteous, eyed me in a $\boxed{\textit{way}}$
    That made me think he wished I wouldn't stay.

32. The moon, Dolores, orbiting the $\boxed{\textit{earth}}$,
    Shines in Peoria as well as Perth.

33. No belle a $\boxed{\textit{novel}}$ reads in bed.
    She plays another game instead.

34. I'm weary of the mawkish songs you sing,
    And $\boxed{\textit{very}}$ weary of no wedding ring.

35. Each noon Collette has lunch with all the frills,
    But $\boxed{\textit{never}}$ thinks of picking up the bills.

36. Darling, you who have so much $\boxed{\textit{to give}}$,
    Give me the right to share the life you live.

37. We all know Bee spoke up today in church.
    She claimed the $\boxed{\textit{bishop}}$ left her in the lurch.

38. Moe, hoe neatly the garden bed.
    The boss has an $\boxed{\textit{eye}}$ in the back of his head.

39. Joe, row harder! I've been told
    The caves we seek are lined with $\boxed{\textit{gold}}$.

40. While you $\boxed{\textit{'re}}$ intent on $\boxed{\textit{playing}}$ soccer
    I'll guard the guy who guards your locker.

41. Your frumpy elegance, your ravaged $\boxed{\textit{skin}}$
    Speak of a lifelong battle lost to gin.

42. Pray, goon, taboo these senseless queries,
    Like $\boxed{\textit{questions}}$ on the next World Series.

43. Myra, Easter seals bring in the loot
    That helps attack diseases at the ⌈ *root* ⌉ .

44. Today I see a ray of hope:
    Our ⌈ *king* ⌉ has been elected pope.

45. We grope around the cave, although with loathing
    We feel the squeaking bats invade our ⌈ *clothing* ⌉ .

46. Sol told Sal she knows not God because
    She's never made the ⌈ *leap* ⌉ from Santa Claus.

47. Where castles ⌈ *centuries* ⌉ old look down on one
    The sea glows faintly in the setting sun.

48. Sole heir to Grandmother's estate,
    I ⌈ *am accustomed* ⌉ just to watch and wait.

49. I swear Tecumseh was my earliest master.
    He taught me ⌈ *luck* ⌉ will favor him who's faster.

50. The star, they say, came to the party ⌈ *late* ⌉ .
    Her friends took off and left her to her fate.

Glossary

English	Spanish
able, be (v.)	poder
above (adv.)	encima
according to (prep.)	según
account (n.)	cuenta
accustomed to, be (v.)	soler
acquaintance (n.)	conocimiento
add (v.)	agregar
advice (n.)	consejo
affair (n.)	asunto
affection (n.)	cariño
after (prep.)	trás (de)
afternoon (adv., noun)	tarde
against (prep.)	contra
agent (n.)	agente
agree (v.)	convenir
agreement (n.)	acuerdo
air (n.)	aire
alien (adj.)	ajeno, -a
alive (adj.)	vivo, -a
all the way to (adv.)	hasta
allow (v.)	dejar
almost (adv.)	casi
alone (adj.)	solo, -a
along (prep.)	por
also (adv.)	también
although (conj.)	aunque

always (adv.)	siempre
among (prep.)	entre
anger (n.)	cólera
another (adj.)	otro, -a
answer (v.)	contestar
anxiety (n.)	ansia
appear (v.)	parecer
appearance (n.)	aspecto
appointment (n.)	cita
arm (body part) (n.)	brazo
arm (weapon) (n.)	arma
arrest (v.)	detener
arrive (v.)	llegar
arrogant (adj.)	soberbio, -a
ascertain (v.)	averiguar
ash, ashes (n.)	ceniza
ask (a question) (v.)	preguntar
ask for (v.)	pedir
at (prep.)	en
at once (adv.)	en seguida
at present (adv.)	actualmente
attend (v.)	asistir
attitude (n.)	ademán
avenge (v.)	vengar
back (adv.)	atrás
back (n.)	espalda
badly (adv.)	mal
bank (of river) (n.)	ribera
bathe (v.)	bañar
be (v.)	estar
beard (n.)	barba
beat (v.)	batir
beautiful (adj.)	hermoso, -a
bed (n.)	cama
beg (v.)	rogar
begin (v.)	empezar
begin to appear (v.)	asomar
behind (adv.)	atrás, detrás de
behind (prep.)	trás (de)
believe (v.)	creer
beloved (adj.)	querido, -a
below (adv.)	abajo
better (adj.)	mejor
between (prep.)	entre

beyond (prep.)	trás (de)
big (adj.)	enorme
bill (n.)	cuenta
bird (n.)	ave
bishop (n.)	obispo
black (adj.)	negro, -a
bless (v.)	bendecir
blind (adj.)	ciego, -a
blood (n.)	sangre
blow (n.)	golpe
blue (adj.)	azul
boat (n.)	barco
body (n.)	cuerpo
boil (v.)	hervir
bone (n.)	hueso
book (n.)	libro
border (n.)	borde
born, be (v.)	nacer
boss (n.)	jefe
both (adj.)	ambos, -as
bother (n.)	enojo
bottom (n.)	fondo
box (n.)	caja
boy (n.)	mozo, niño
boyfriend (n.)	novio
branch (n.)	rama
branch (small) (n.)	ramo
bread (n.)	pan
break (v.)	quebrar, romper
breast (n.)	pecho
breath (n.)	aliento
breed (n.)	raza
bring (v.)	traer
broken (adj.)	quebrado
brother (n.)	hermano
bud (v.)	brotar
burden (n.)	cargo
burn (v.)	arder, quemar
burst (v.)	estallar
business (n.)	asunto
but (conj.)	pero, sino
call (v.)	llamar
campus (n.)	campo
can (v.)	poder

cane (n.)	palo
capable (adj.)	capaz
car (n.)	carro, coche
carelessness (n.)	descuido
carry (v.)	llevar
case (n.)	caso
cede (v.)	ceder
century (n.)	siglo
certain (adj.)	cierto, -a, seguro, -a
chamber (n.)	cámara
change (n.)	moneda
change (v.)	cambiar
cheese (n.)	queso
chest (n.)	pecho
chew (v.)	mascar
chief (n.)	jefe
choose (v.)	elegir, escoger
chunk (n.)	trozo
claim (v.)	reclamar
clash (v.)	chocar
class (n.)	clase
clear (adj.)	claro, -a
climb (v.)	escalar, subir
cloak (n.)	manto
close (v.)	cerrar
cloth (n.)	tela
clothes, clothing (n.)	ropa, vestido
clumsy (adj.)	torpe
coach (n.)	coche, carro
coast (n.)	costa
coin (n.)	moneda
cold (adj.)	frío, -a
collect (v.)	cobrar, recoger
collide (v.)	chocar
come (v.)	venir
come into view (v.)	asomar
comfort (n.)	consuelo
command (n.)	orden
command (v.)	mandar
commission (n.)	encargo
commit (v.)	cometer
common (adj.)	corriente
complain (v.)	quejar, reclamar
complaint (n.)	queja
conceal (v.)	ocultar

concise (adj.)	preciso, -a
conduct (v.)	conducir
conquer (v.)	vencer
consolation (n.)	consuelo
contained, be (v.)	caber
contempt (n.)	desprecio
continue (v.)	proseguir
cook (v.)	cocer
correct (adj.)	justo, -a
cost (n.)	costa
counsel (n.)	consejo
count (v.)	contar
countenance (n.)	figura, rostro
country (fatherland) (n.)	país
country (rural area) (n.)	campo
courage (n.)	aliento
course (n.)	rumbo
court (n.)	corte
cousin (n.)	primo, -a
cover (v.)	cubrir, tapar
cover up (v.)	tapar
crack (v.)	partir
crime (n.)	delito
cross (n.)	cruz
cross (v.)	atravesar, cruzar
crown (n.)	corona
crush (v.)	hundir
crying (n.)	llanto
current (adj.)	corriente
custom (n.)	estilo
cut (v.)	cortar
damage (n.)	daño
dance (v.)	bailar
danger (n.)	peligro
dare (v.)	atreverse, osar
date (appointment) (n.)	cita
date (calendar) (n.)	fecha
dawn (n.)	aurora
day (n.)	día
dealings (n.)	trato
dear (adj.)	querido, -a
debt (n.)	deber
deceive (v.)	engañar
deed (n.)	hecho

defeat (v.)	vencer
degree (n.)	grado
demand (v.)	exigir, reclamar
deny (v.)	negar
depend (v.)	depender
deprive (v.)	privar
depth (n.)	fondo
descend (v.)	bajar
deserve (v.)	merecer
desire (n.)	deseo
desire (v.)	desear, querer
detain (v.)	detener
die (v.)	morir
different (adj.)	nuevo, -a
direct (v.)	dirigir
direction (n.)	rumbo
disdain (n.)	desprecio
do (v.)	hacer
dog (n.)	perro
door (n.)	puerta
doubt (n.)	duda
down (adv.)	abajo
drain (v.)	agotar
draw (curtains) (v.)	tirar
dream (n.)	sueño
dream (v.)	soñar
dress (n.)	vestido
dress (v.)	vestir
drink (v.)	beber
drop (n.)	gota
drown (v.)	ahogar
dry (adj.)	seco, -a
dry (v.)	secar
dull (adj.)	torpe
during (prep.)	durante
dust (n.)	polvo
duty (n.)	deber
earn (v.)	ganar
earth (n.)	mundo
easy (adj.)	fácil
eat (v.)	comer
edge (n.)	borde
egg (n.)	huevo
either (adv.)	tampoco

elect (v.)	elegir
elevate (v.)	alzar
embrace (n.)	abrazo
empty (adj.)	vacío, -a
enchantment (n.)	encanto
encircle (v.)	rodear
end (n.)	fin
enjoy (v.)	gozar, gustar
enough, be (v.)	bastar
entire (adj.)	entero, -a
envy (v.)	envidiar
epoch (n.)	época
erase (v.)	borrar
every (adj.)	todo, -a
exact (adj.)	justo, -a, preciso, -a
excuse (v.)	disculpar
exercise (v.)	ejercer
exhaust (v.)	agotar
expect (v.)	esperar
explode (v.)	estallar
eye (n.)	ojo
face (n.)	cara, rostro
fact (n.)	hecho
faith (n.)	fe
faithful (adj.)	fiel
fall (v.)	caer
far (adv.)	lejos
fasten (v.)	cerrar, prender
fat (adj.)	gordo, -a
fear (n.)	susto
fear (v.)	temer
feature (n.)	rasgo
feed (v.)	alimentar
feel, feel sorry (v.)	sentir
field (n.)	campo
fight (n.)	lucha
fight (v.)	luchar
figure (n.)	figura
fill (v.)	llenar
find (v.)	hallar
find out (v.)	averiguar
fine (adv.)	bien
finger (n.)	dedo
fire (n.)	fuego

fish (n.)	pez
fit, fit into (v.)	caber
fix (v.)	fijar
flee (v.)	huir
fly (v.)	volar
follow (v.)	seguir, suceder
following (adj.)	siguiente
food (n.)	alimento
foot (n.)	pie
for (prep.)	para
force (n.)	fuerza
foreign (adj.)	ajeno, -a
foreigner (n.)	extranjero, -a
forest (n.)	bosque
forget (v.)	olvidar
forgetfulness (n.)	olvido
forward! (adv.)	adelante
fountain (n.)	fuente
free (adj.)	libre
freeze (v.)	helar
friend (n.)	amigo
frighten (v.)	asustar
from the (prep.)	del, de la
fruit (n.)	fruta
full (adj.)	lleno, -a, pleno, -a
future (n.)	porvenir
game (n.)	juego
garden (n.)	huerta
gather (v.)	recoger
generous (adj.)	gentil
genius (n.)	ingenio
gentle (adj.)	gentil
German (n.)	alemán, -mana
gesture (n.)	ademán
get off (v.)	bajar
give (v.)	dar
glass (drinking) (n.)	vaso
go (v).	ir
go ahead! (v.)	adelante
god (n.)	dios
gold (n.)	oro
good-bye (n.)	adiós
good fortune (n.)	dicha
goodness (n.)	bondad

go through (v.)	recorrer
go to bed (v.)	acostarse
go up (v.)	subir
govern (v.)	mandar
grace (n.)	sal
grandfather, grandpa (n.)	abuelo
grandson (n.)	nieto
grave (adj.)	grave
gravy (n.)	salsa
greater (adj.)	mayor
green (adj.)	verde
greet (v.)	acoger
grow (v.)	crecer
guarantee (v.)	fiar
guide (v.)	guiar
guilt (n.)	culpa
gun (n.)	arma
hair (n.)	pelo
half (adj.)	medio, -a
hall (n.)	cámara
hand (n.)	mano
handwriting (n.)	letra
hang (v.)	colgar
happen (v.)	pasar, suceder
happy (adj.)	alegre, dichoso, -a, feliz
harbor (n.)	puerto
harbor (v.)	acoger
hard (adj.)	duro, -a
hardly (adv.)	apenas
haste (n.)	prisa
hate (n.)	odio
have just (v.)	acabar de
he (pron.)	él
head (n.)	cabeza
hear (v.)	oír
heart (n.)	corazón
hearth (n.)	hogar
heat (n.)	calor
heaven (n.)	cielo
here (adv.)	aquí
here is (v.)	he aquí
hide (v.)	ocultar
hit upon (v.)	acertar
holy (adj.)	santo, -a

home (n.)	hogar
honey (n.)	miel
hope (n.)	esperanza
hope, hope for (v.)	esperar
hour (n.)	hora
house (n.)	casa
how (adv.)	cómo
however (adv.)	sin embargo
hug (n.)	abrazo
huge (adj.)	enorme
human (adj.)	humano, -a
humid (adj.)	húmedo, -a
humor (n.)	sal
hunger (n.)	hambre
hurl (v.)	lanzar
hurry (v.)	apurar
hurt (v.)	herir
husband (n.)	esposo
ice (n.)	hielo
idea (n.)	idea
ill (adj.)	enfermo, -a
in (prep.)	en
in back of (adv.)	detrás de
in case (conj.)	caso
income (n.)	renta
increase (n.)	aumento
inform (v.)	enterar
inhale (v.)	aspirar
in jail (adv.)	preso, -a
in order to (prep.)	para
inquire (v.)	preguntar
insane (adj.)	loco, -a
inside (adv.)	adentro
insist (v.)	exigir
invent (v.)	inventar
iron (n.)	hierro
jail (n.)	cárcel
jealousy (n.)	celos
job (n.)	empleo
joke (n.)	broma, burla
joy (n.)	dicha
judge (n.)	juez
judge (v.)	juzgar

judgment (n.)	juicio
juice (n.)	zumo
kill (v.)	matar
kind (adj.)	gentil
kindle (v.)	encender
kindness (n.)	bondad
king (n.)	rey
kiss (n.)	beso
kiss (v.)	besar
kitchen (n.)	cocina
know (v.)	saber
lake (n.)	lago
land (n.)	tierra
landlord (n.)	amo
large (adj.)	enorme
larger (adj.)	mayor
late (adv.)	tarde
laugh (n.)	risa
laugh (v.)	reír
laughter (n.)	risa
law (n.)	ley
lay out (v.)	tender
lazy (adj.)	perezoso, -a
lead (v.)	conducir
leaf (n.)	hoja
leap (n.)	salto
learn (v.)	aprender
leave (v.)	quitar
leave (behind) (v.)	dejar
leg (n.)	pierna
lend (v.)	prestar
less (adj.)	menos
letter (correspondence) (n.)	carta
letter (of alphabet) (n.)	letra
lie (n.)	mentira
lie (v.)	mentir
life (n.)	vida
light (adj.)	ligero, -a
light (n.)	luz
light (v.)	encender
light-colored (adj.)	claro, -a
like (adj.)	semejante

like (v.)	gustar, querer
lineage (n.)	raza
list (n.)	lista
listen, listen to (v.)	escuchar
little (quantity) (adj.)	poco, -a
live (v.)	vivir
living (adj.)	vivo, -a
load (n.)	cargo
loan (v.)	prestar
lock (v.)	cerrar
long (adj.)	largo, -a
look after (v.)	cuidar
look at (v.)	mirar
look for (v.)	buscar
loosen (v.)	soltar
lose (v.)	perder
loss (n.)	daño
love (n.)	amor, cariño
love (v.)	amar, querer
low (adj.)	bajo, -a
loyal (adj.)	fiel
luck (n.)	suerte, ventura
mad (adj.)	loco, -a
madness (n.)	locura
maintain, support (v.)	sostener
make (v.)	hacer
make a mistake (v.)	equivocar
man (n.)	hombre
manner (n.)	manera
mantle (n.)	manto
Mass (n.)	misa
master (n.)	amo, maestro
meal (n.)	comida
measure, measurement (n.)	medida
meat (n.)	carne
memory (n.)	recuerdo
merry (adj.)	alegre
mien (n.)	figura
mind (n.)	mente
mine (pron.)	mío, -a
mirror (n.)	espejo
mistake (v.)	equivocar
mix (v.)	mezclar, revolver

mock (v.)	burlar
moment (n.)	rato
money (n.)	dinero, moneda
month (n.)	mes
more (adv.)	más
morning (n.)	mañana
mount (v.)	subir
mountain (n.)	montaña
mournful (adj.)	doloroso, -a
mouth (n.)	boca
much (adj.)	mucho, -a
mute (adj.)	mudo, -a
name (n.)	nombre
near (adv.)	cerca
necessary (adj.)	preciso, -a
need (v.)	requerir
neglect (n.)	descuido
neighbor (n.)	vecino
neither (adj.)	tampoco
neither . . . nor (conj.)	ni . . . ni
nervous (adj.)	nervioso, -a
never (adv.)	jamás, nunca
nevertheless (adv.)	sin embargo
new (adj.)	nuevo, -a
news (n.)	noticias
next (adj.)	siguiente
night (n.)	noche
no one (pron.)	nadie
nor (conj.)	tampoco
note (v.)	notar
not either (adv.)	tampoco
nothing (pron.)	nada
novel (n.)	novela
now (adv.)	ahora
nowadays (adv.)	actualmente
object (n.)	objeto
occur (v.)	pasar, suceder
of mine (adj.)	mío, -a
of the (prep.)	del, de la
oil (n.)	aceite
old (adj.)	viejo, -a
old age (n.)	vejez
on (prep.)	en, sobre

only (adj.)	único, -a
open (v.)	abrir
oppress	oprimir
orchard (n.)	huerta
order (n.)	encargo, orden
order (v.)	mandar
other (adj.)	otro, -a
out, outside (adv.)	fuera
oversight (n.)	olvido
own (adj.)	propio, -a
owner (n.)	amo
page (n.)	hoja
pain (n.)	dolor, pena
painting (n.)	pintura
paper (n.)	papel
parlor (n.)	cámara
pass (v.)	pasar
pay (v.)	pagar
peace (n.)	paz
people (n.)	gente
perform (v.)	ejercer
perhaps (adv.)	acaso, tal vez
person (n.)	sujeto
person apprehended (n.)	preso, -a
petting (n.)	caricia
pick up (v.)	recoger
picture (n.)	pintura
piece (n.)	trozo
place (n.)	lugar, sitio
place (v.)	colocar, poner
plaint (n.)	queja
play (v.)	jugar
play (musical instrument) (v.)	tocar
plead (v.)	rogar
please (v.)	placer
pleasure (n.)	gusto
point (n.)	punto
poor (adj.)	pobre
port (n.)	puerto
possess (v.)	poseer
pound (n.)	libra
pour (v.)	echar
poverty (n.)	pobreza

praise (v.)	alabar
pray (v.)	rezar, rogar
preach (v.)	predicar
precise (adj.)	preciso, -a
prepare (v.)	prevenir
present, be (v.)	asistir
press (v.)	apurar, oprimir
pretend (v.)	fingir
pretty (adj.)	bonito, -a
prick (v.)	picar
prize (n.)	premio
probe (v.)	probar
proceed (v.)	proseguir
prompt (adj.)	pronto
proof (n.)	prueba
prove (v.)	probar
pull (v.)	tirar
push (v.)	empujar
queen (n.)	reina
question (n.)	pregunta
quickly (adv.)	pronto
race (contest) (n.)	carrera
race (breed) (n.)	raza
raise (v.)	alzar
reach (a place) (v.)	alcanzar
read (v.)	leer
ready (adj.)	pronto
receive (v.)	acoger
red (adj.)	rojo, -a
refuse (v.)	negar
regress (v.)	regresar
remembrance (n.)	recuerdo
rend (v.)	partir
rent (n.)	renta
repent (v.)	arrepentirse
replace (v.)	reponer
reply (v.)	contestar
request (v.)	pedir
require (v.)	requerir
resolution (n.)	acuerdo
restore (v.)	reponer
return (v.)	regresar, volver
revenge (v.)	vengar

revenue (n.)	renta
reward (n.)	premio
river (n.)	río
road (n.)	camino
rob (v.)	robar
rock (n.)	roca
room (n.)	pieza
root (n.)	raíz
rouse (v.)	conmover
royal (adj.)	real
rule (n.)	regla
run (v.)	correr
sad (adj.)	doloroso, -a, triste
safe (adj.)	seguro, -a
saintly (adj.)	santo, -a
salary (n.)	sueldo
salt (n.)	sal
same (adj.)	mismo, -a
sample (n.)	muestra
sauce (n.)	salsa
save (v.)	salvar
say (v.)	decir
scale (v.)	escalar
scarcely (adv.)	apenas
school (n.)	escuela
scoff (v.)	burlar
scream (v.)	gritar
screen (n.)	tela
sea (n.)	mar
search (n.)	busca
seat (n.)	asiento
seat (v.)	sentar
see (v.)	ver
seek (v.)	buscar
seem (v.)	parecer
seize (v.)	prender
sell on credit (v.)	fiar
send (v.)	enviar, mandar
separate (v.)	apartar
serious (adj.)	grave, serio, -a
servant (n.)	criado
serve (v.)	servir
set (v.)	colocar, poner
shake (v.)	temblar

shame (n.)	vergüenza
shape (n.)	figura
shelter (v.)	acoger
ship (n.)	barco
shiver (v.)	temblar
shocking, be (v.)	chocar
shoe (n.)	zapato
shoot (v.)	tirar
shore (n.)	ribera
short (adj.)	bajo, -a
shoulder (n.)	hombro
shout (v.)	gritar
shudder (v.)	temblar
sick (adj.)	enfermo, -a
sidewalk (n.)	acera
sigh (n.)	suspiro
sign (n.)	muestra
sign (v.)	firmar
silent (adj.)	mudo, -a
silk (n.)	seda
similar (adj.)	semejante
simple (adj.)	sencillo, -a
sin (n.)	pecado
sing (v.)	cantar
sink (v.)	hundir
size (n.)	medida
skin (n.)	piel
sky (n.)	cielo
sleep (v.)	dormir
smoke (n.)	humo
so (adv.)	así
sober (adj.)	grave, serio, -a
some (adj.)	alguno, -a
something (n.)	algo
son (n.)	hijo
song (n.)	canto
son-in-law (n.)	yerno
soon (adv.)	pronto
sorrow (n.)	pena
soul (n.)	alma
sound (v.)	sonar
source (n.)	fuente
speak (v.)	hablar
speed up (v.)	apurar
spend (v.)	gastar

sphere (n.)	esfera
split (v.)	partir
spray (n.)	ramo
sprig (n.)	ramo
spring (n.)	fuente
squeeze (v.)	apretar
standard (adj.)	corriente
start (v.)	empezar
steer (v.)	dirigir
step (n.)	paso
stick (n.)	palo
still (adv.)	todavía
sting (v.)	picar
stir (v.)	revolver
stop (v.)	detener, parar
stop up (v.)	tapar
store (n.)	tienda
straight (adj.)	recto, -a
stranger (n.)	extranjero
strength (n.)	fuerza
stretch, stretch out (v.)	tender
strip (n.)	lista
stripe (n.)	lista
struggle (v.)	luchar
study (v.)	estudiar
stupid (adj.)	torpe
style (n.)	estilo
subdue (v.)	sujetar
subject (n.)	sujeto
subway (n.)	metro
success (n.)	éxito
such (adj.)	tal
suffering (n.)	pena
sugar (n.)	azúcar
suit (n.)	vestido
sum (n.)	suma
summer (n.)	verano
sun (n.)	sol
supper (n.)	cena
support (v.)	apoyar, sostener
suppose (v.)	suponer
sure (adj.)	seguro, -a
surround (v.)	rodear
sustain (v.)	sostener
swear (v.)	jurar

tablet (n.)	tabla
take (v.)	llevar, prender, tomar
take advantage of (v.)	aprovechar
take care of (v.)	cuidar
take out (v.)	sacar
talk (v.)	hablar
taste (n.)	gusto
taste (v.)	estar
teacher (n.)	maestro
tell (v.)	decir
tender (adj.)	tierno, -a
tenderness (n.)	caricia, ternura
test (v.)	probar
that (over yonder) (adj.)	aquel
then (adv.)	entonces, luego
there (adv.)	ahí, allí
thing (n.)	cosa
think (v.)	creer, hallar, pensar
though (conj.)	aunque
thousand (n.)	mil
thread (n.)	hilo
threaten (v.)	amenazar
through (prep.)	por
throw (v.)	arrojar, echar, lanzar
thus (adv.)	así
tie, tie up (v.)	atar
time (n.)	época
time (series) (n.)	vez
tire (v.)	cansar
today (adv.)	hoy
toe (n.)	dedo
together (adv.)	junto, -a
tomorrow (adv.)	mañana
too (adv.)	también
touch (v.)	tocar
tough (adj.)	duro, -a
toward (prep.)	hacia
tower (n.)	torre
town (n.)	pueblo
trace (v.)	trazar
trade (n.)	oficio, trato
trait (n.)	rasgo
transport (v.)	llevar
traverse (v.)	recorrer
treat (v.)	tratar

treatment (n.)	trato
tree (n.)	árbol
tremble (v.)	temblar
trial (n.)	juicio
trick (n.)	burla
trick (v.)	engañar
trip (n.)	viaje
trouble (n.)	enojo
troop (n.)	tropa
trust (v.)	fiar
try (v.)	probar
turn off (v.)	apagar
turn over (v.)	revolver
ugly (adj.)	feo, -a
uncle (n.)	tío
understand (v.)	entender
untie (v.)	soltar
until (adv.)	hasta
up (adv.)	arriba
upon (prep.)	sobre
upstairs (adv.)	arriba
value (n.)	valor
vapor (n.)	humo
verge (n.)	borde
very (adv.)	muy
vice (n.)	vicio
view (n.)	vista
visage (n.)	rostro
voice (n.)	voz
void (adj.)	vacío, -a
wait, wait for (v.)	esperar
waiter (n.)	mozo
waken (v.)	despertar
walk (v.)	andar
want (v.)	desear, querer
war (n.)	guerra
warmth (n.)	calor
warn (v.)	prevenir
waste (v.)	gastar
watch (v.)	mirar
water (n.)	agua

wave (n.)	ola
way (n.)	manera, modo
weapon (n.)	arma
wear (v.)	llevar
web (n.)	tela
wedding (n.)	boda
week (n.)	semana
weigh (v.)	pesar
weight (n.)	peso
well (adv.)	bien
wheat (n.)	trigo
where (adv.)	dónde
which (adj.)	cuál
while (adv.)	mientras
while (n.)	rato
white (adj.)	blanco, -a
whole (adj.)	entero, -a
why (adv.)	por qué
wide (adj.)	ancho, -a
widower (n.)	viudo
win (v.)	ganar
wind (n.)	viento
wing (n.)	ala
wise (adj.)	sabio, -a
wish (v.)	desear, querer
wit (n.)	sal
without (prep.)	sin
woman (n.)	mujer
woods (n.)	bosque
wool (n.)	lana
work (v.)	trabajar
work, work of art (n.)	obra
world (n.)	mundo
worth (n.)	valor
worth, be (v.)	valer
wound (n.)	herida
wound (v.)	herir
wrath (n.)	ira
write (v.)	escribir
year (n.)	año
yesterday (adv.)	ayer
yet (adv.)	todavía
yield (v.)	ceder

young (adj.)	joven
youth (n.)	juventud
zeal (n.)	afán